greatrenovations

a new life for old houses

Mary Gilliatt

greatrenovations

a new life for old houses

For my dear friend, Mary Cookson,
as inspirational a renovator as she is painter
and, not least, person.

First published in 2003 by Conran Octopus Limited,
a part of Octopus Publishing Group, 2–4 Heron Quays,
London E14 4JP
www.conran-octopus.co.uk

Text copyright © Mary Gilliatt 2003
Design and layout copyright © Conran Octopus 2003

The right of Mary Gilliatt to be identified as Author of this
Work has been asserted by her in accordance with the
Copyright, Designs and Patents Act 1998.

Publishing Director: Lorraine Dickey
Senior Editor: Katey Day
Project Editor: Helen Ridge
Art Director: Chi Lam
Designer: Mary Staples
Picture Research: Rachel Davies
Production Manager: Angela Couchman
Production Assistant: Natalie Moore

British Cataloguing-in-Publication Data.
A catalogue record for this book is available from
the British Library.

ISBN 1 84091 299 5

Printed and bound in China

contents

The renovation and revival of old houses is a thriving industry.
It is the housing equivalent of having your cake and eating it too,
because with careful planning you can combine the charm of the
old with the best of the new.

CHAPTER ONE

Beyond the aesthetic and nostalgic pleasures inherent in
the revival of older houses there are many obvious benefits.
Abandoned, unloved spaces with a minimum of modern
comforts can be offputting, but bringing an old house back
to life is a rewarding experience.

CHAPTER TWO

Before embarking on renovation work, it is essential to
understand the historical context of your building.

introduction

The renovation industry – and it is now an industry – is thriving. It is not hard to see why this now-global industry continues to burgeon. From the 1920s until the 1970s, many people wanted the new at all costs, yet to the distress of architects, most seemed to prefer their 'new' served up as rather poor reproductions – pastiches of 17th-, 18th- or early 19th-century façades, and sometimes a mixture of two or three, fronting more convenient contemporary assemblages of rooms. What people rarely wanted, it appears, was to preserve, maintain or revive the genuinely old. As a result, far too many formerly splendid structures, historic public buildings, as well as charming domestic dwellings in all shapes, sizes and situations, were torn down or left to rot and collapse on their own.

After World War II, what had not been achieved by bombs and shells was largely wrought by insensitivity and sheer carelessness, quite as much as by lack of money, or will, for restoration. But for the past 30 years or so, more and more people, alarmed by ugly urban sprawl, and, for the most part, uglier new housing developments, have finally seen the advantages of saving and reviving the best, or the sturdiest, of the old. Moreover, the global success of companies like Ralph Lauren that have built their entire marketing strategy on the back of a perceived nostalgia for a more gracious past, has certainly filtered through to the housing market, as well as decoration in general. 'Old is the New New' and 'Old is the New Chic' run the coverlines on homes and interiors magazines and headlines on lifestyle pages. Discovering and reintroducing old mores as well as old designs; old architectural details and old buildings as well as antique furniture and old recipes, has become a kind of international, early 21st-century treasure hunt. Salvage yards, architectural features depots, antiques shops and antiques fairs have proliferated in countless countries.

This trend is not simply a search for the best and most distinguished, at least in the housing arena. Many people, lured back to city living for the ease of getting to work, or for better schools, shops, restaurants and entertainment, are snapping up old terrace houses, town houses and workers' cottages in formerly down-at-heel areas. Quite apart from the inevitable upgrading of the neighbourhoods that this triggers, they then transform the often formulaic interiors in ways that would have astonished previous occupants. At the same time older suburban and outer-city dwellings are being bought for relatively low prices – their unique, quirky and, most of all, spacious interiors appealing

greatly to buyers. Meanwhile, people looking for rural peace and quiet, or weekend or holiday homes, are pouncing on old wrecks and run-down buildings in the countryside in unprecedented numbers.

Given this strong and increasingly popular worldwide market for older houses and buildings, it seemed a good idea to provide an international sourcebook of ideas for renovating and decorating the different house types, of different periods, in different countries and different continents. By this I mean urban and suburban houses, rural houses, holiday homes, and buildings that can be converted into homes, such as churches, chapels, old schools, barns, industrial lofts and even garages.

For the purposes of this book it seemed best to define old and older houses as any domestic or convertible building built between the 16th and 17th centuries and the 1950s. *Old* houses, or period houses, are those built up to the end of the 19th century, while *older* houses are those built in the 20th century up to the 1950s. There are not too many extant *entire* houses that were built before the late 16th century, although many people claim, not often correctly, exceptionally early provenance for their buildings. It is reasonable to say, however, that many old houses do contain within them much earlier bits and pieces to a greater or lesser degree, and that sometimes they are sitting on much older foundations. So it is helpful to be able to recognize these elements if you come across them. Because of the huge demand for new houses after the end of World War II, and because of new materials and advances in prefabricated parts, old building methods changed substantially, hence the 1950s cut-off date.

There are many practical, well-illustrated and thoroughly useful books on the nuts and bolts of renovation and restoration and on older houses in general. But in my very long experience of the decorating and housing world, what anyone wants to extrapolate from any book on the design and decorating of houses are good and appealing ideas. People generally need the inspiration for what to do in the first place before finding out how to achieve it. And most of us could certainly use the extra bolstering of confidence needed before embarking on any older house project, whatever its age. Should you, for example, keep to the apparent spirit of the house come what may, or do what best suits your lifestyle – and, of course, pocket? How far should you go with repairs and restoration? Should you respect the period or style of the house in the renovation, furnishings and colour schemes, or presume that past builders and owners would have made quite different decisions had they had the choice of materials, plumbing, heating and air-conditioning, lighting, colours, furniture and fabrics

that we enjoy today? Should you strip away all the layers imposed by former generations to reveal the original workmanship, or might that prove disastrous? How can you become reasonably sensitive to all the various period styles and understand how they evolved? Dare you try to dig out old floors in a really old house or cottage in order to gain an extra inch of headroom, or might that make the probably meagre foundations collapse?

All of these initial concerns, and more, face the new old-house owner hoping to make as good and sensitive a job as possible of its renovation. I have therefore tried here to address these and similar questions, as well as to show interesting interiors of different nationalities that can be adapted or used as starting points for similar types and periods of houses in similar situations. Most particularly, I have tried to show innovative renovations achieved by owners, or their architects and designers, who have used the bones of their respective buildings, so to speak, as a springboard for new and impressive uses for the given space, or for ingenious additions or transformations. The very many ways, in short, to give a new, vigorous and imaginative life to old buildings without – and this is crucial to all lovers of old houses – in any way forgoing their original character.

why renovate?

1

The repair and renovation of

any historic building will be a

rewarding and responsible

undertaking – and more often

than not a time-consuming

and complicated one. The

necessary level of work can

vary greatly from light cosmetic

renovation to a complete

overhaul of the building. Those

who embark on such a project

often find that the work is as

enriching as it is challenging.

left

The 19th-century overmantel mirror resting on the mantel shelf, the ornamental mouldings and interestingly shaped tops to the shelves (effecting a somewhat Gothic look) give a historical feel to this dining room. In contrast, the grey paintwork, furnishings and the neat glass-fronted cupboards below the shelves give it a more contemporary edge.

right

When designer Bruce Oldfield first saw the 18th-century mill house that he has since restored, this now spacious-looking area had dark brown-painted beams and dark red brick walls, while the gallery was so close to the ceiling it was impossible to stand upright. The makeover involved lowering the gallery a little and painting most of the beams and woodwork a freshening off-white. The transformation is remarkable in every way.

first impressions

It is easy to be enchanted by really old houses that have been well kept or sensitively restored, or at least look quite capable of being restored and renovated. It is also easy to be captivated by their atmosphere inside and out, the sense of age, the beauty of ancient walls and windows and dipping roofs, the worn and weathered stones or bricks or clapboard, the mellowed and faded colours. What is not so easy is to see the possible merits in other old houses and buildings that at first inspection seem to have little potential.

For every stunning old house, there are many more that look dreary, dilapidated and depressing; rundown if not ruined, or at least ruinously expensive to improve. And there are thousands more that are elderly rather than really old. Nevertheless, most old houses deserve a second, much more searching examination. I have heard so many stories of people not even wanting to go inside some apparently bleak little wreck, only to ask to go back later. The outside might look battered and unloved; the wiring, plumbing, drainage and central heating might be practically nonexistent; kitchens and bathrooms pathetic; the decoration ghastly; the last owner's attempts at modernization a disaster; and the arrangements of rooms the antithesis of what you thought you wanted. Yet, on reflection, there was something about that house…

left

Most of the plaster on the walls of this small dining room was removed to reveal the stonework underneath. The stones were then tidied up with new grouting where necessary. The rest of the room has also been pared down, with the floorboards stripped and stained a distinguished brownish-black, the beams exposed and the window left uncovered.

right

The unusual panelling of this late 19th-century home leads the eye up to the ceiling. Careful paintwork makes the most of the carpentry, while the polished wooden floor continues the theme.

the advantages

If you can get past first impressions, the most dilapidated of older houses may have a hidden potential. Even if it is not at first discernible because of the off-putting tangle of weeds and brush, a great many older houses and buildings sit on mature sites with mature trees. Gardens have often been planned and planted and tended over many years. No matter if they have been woefully untended for some time, they are generally capable of not only being brought back to their former charm, but also of yielding unexpected pleasures along the way – plants and shrubs that would take years to cultivate around a new house. Quite apart from the site, unattractively rendered outside walls might be found to mask a very different house underneath, in old stone perhaps, or bricks, or even lath and plaster.

Inside old houses, the walls are generally very solid, even if currently cracked, damp and dripping. There are sometimes beautiful old floors to restore under a tatty carpet or stained linoleum; interesting mouldings, cornices and dados, blocked-up fireplaces or stone niches underneath the peeling, dirty wallpaper or ravaged, dark-hued paint. If you are really lucky, you could even uncover long-concealed panelling. Windows might be basically elegant, even if they are half-broken and rotting. Millwork or woodwork and doors can also prove far more handsome than previously thought, under the thick layers of dirt and paint that have obliterated the original design. And rooms are often better proportioned and more spacious than those in run-of-the-mill modern houses – a fact that might not be immediately apparent because of a maze of flimsy partition walls that were put up at some stage in the past. So look carefully when considering renovation work – you may well find a wealth of hidden charms.

the disadvantages

Many people are put off renovating old houses because of the near-inevitable work and time required for the restoration and replacement of the fabric of the building, as well as the installation or renewal of essentials, such as up-to-standard wiring, lighting, plumbing, heating, insulation and good bathrooms and kitchens. But, given the budget and the commitment, these are comparatively easy problems to resolve, and in the case of the bathrooms and kitchens a lot can be achieved by simple cosmetic touches.

Very different challenges, of course, are presented by the legacy of previous occupants who, anxious to modernize, have left walls smoothed to nonentity, chimneys blocked up, mantelpieces removed, mouldings torn away, graceful old windows and doors replaced by plate glass picture windows, and original floors and tiles covered by vinyl.

Ironically, just as bad are the problems caused by enthusiastic but uninformed 'restorers' who, however knowledgeable they were about buildings in general, either lacked the proper sensitivity to old buildings or imperfectly understood their period or character. Instead of faithful copies in the right materials, you might find old brick and stone crudely repointed; a mixture of either unsightly reproduction bow or regular windows with bull's-eye panes, or so-called 'Georgian' sash windows with the wrong number and width of glazing bars; front doors with built-in fanlights that look like those used for cheaper doll's houses; bits of curly wrought iron used for door handles and light switches, and several other crude reproductions.

the pros & cons

As the architect Hugh Lander pointed out in his excellent *The House Restorers' Guide*, it is fortunate that 'any old building must have very serious faults indeed before it becomes either too expensive or too difficult to repair'. This has to be a comforting thought and one that you should be careful to recall if you take on the task of renovating a period house.

Although it may not be immediately apparent, the majority of older houses have more incipient character, idiosyncrasy, architectural detailing and, above all, charm than the average new developments. Your newly acquired period house may need a formidable amount of work doing to it to make it a comfortable place in which to live – this could mean modernizing or installing from scratch the plumbing and wiring, insulation, heating or air-conditioning; replacing windows and window frames, woodwork, roofs or roof tiles and guttering; unblocking chimneys, replacing fireplaces, reorganizing outer and inner walls, and restoring or replacing floors. Yet despite this, it is an undeniably intriguing and rewarding challenge to coax a house and its interior back to its former character. For, all in all, unless you have the means to commission a custom-built house on a carefully chosen and nurtured site, or miraculously happen to find exactly what you want in a speculative house, you are far more likely to achieve your ideal in an older house.

above left

This kitchen combines modernity and practicality within the original beamed framework. Note the old gently arched window with its deep recess that has been left uncovered.

below left

Fitted with a casement window, the attic in this cottage, with its triangular beam structure and sloping roof, makes a cosy bedroom.

above

The 1930s-looking front door appears something of an anachronism in contrast to the steep stone steps, the draught-reducing curtain and the recessed alcove (to the right) of this obviously much older structure.

points to consider

Before beginning to look seriously for an older house, it is as well to have clear in your mind several key points and to be prepared to do some research to discover what you really want. These are elementary preparations that should save you lots of wasted journeys, not to mention helping frustrated owners who all too often have to show their houses to people with absolutely no intention of buying.

It is essential to decide at the outset what would be the ideal shape, size and age of house to renovate, or building to convert, given your budget, timescale and circumstances, and in which area or areas. This may sound obvious but, according to real estate agents, an extraordinary number of would-be buyers do not really think through their needs and preferences. They have not asked themselves whether, for example, they want two bedrooms or four; a house with a small amount of land within easy reach of shops and schools, or one as remote as possible; or whether they would like a terraced cottage or a free-standing one; a town house, a village house or a larger country house with outbuildings and a fair amount of land. Nor have they decided whether they will mind if the house is haphazard or informal rather than architecturally formal and 'correct', or whether they would consider any building in a coveted situation that can be converted into a home, such as a chapel, church, school, barn, pub or inn, mill or suitable industrial building. And if so, how many rooms they would like to end up with, and for what purposes. The 'I'll know it when I see it' attitude is fine if people are wandering around by themselves and have plenty of time, but it is maddening for any agent brought in to help with the venture.

Just as important is to think about services we now mostly take for granted, such as electricity, water, drainage, refuse collections and telephone. If a house is very remote, it might well not have any of these amenities, so substitutes like generator sets,

solar heating or wind power, bored wells, special sanitation or incinerators might have to be arranged if they do not exist, or updated or replaced if they do. Whether you feel up to providing such substitutes or improvements or doing without most amenities except water is something else to make clear to agents. It is astonishing how often these basics are forgotten in the first flush of enthusiasm for a property, just as so many people who should know better forget about wiring and lighting in a house until all the decoration has been completed.

Not only should all these points be clarified early on, and kept in mind as relevant cities, towns, suburbs and parcels of countryside are explored for 'For Sale' signs, but they should also be written down and given to any agent used. They, in turn, should use them as future criteria for assessing which houses to send you details of, and which not.

above

Decorative cast-iron balustrades and pillared supports like these in Louisiana were greatly used in the American South during the 19th century, as they were in Australia.

right

This beautiful 18th-century French stone staircase and balustrade, together with the panelling, have been carefully maintained, without being made to look over-restored.

questions to ask

There are a number of questions you should ask
yourself before buying an old house. First of all,
do you want a true period house? Remember that
a period house usually comes saddled with a whole
host of building regulations that can be restrictive,
not to mention expensive, when it comes to
renovation. Alternatively, would a solidly built,
spacious older house suit you better?

What type of house are you looking for? It could
be a terrace or a detached town house, a village
cottage or house, a country house, some sort of
vacation or holiday home, or a building that you can
convert into a home. And where would you like that
house to be – country, city, town, suburb, village or
remote rural area?

Crucial in terms of financial planning is
establishing a maximum budget that includes the
cost of renovations as well as of house purchase.
To arrive at this you need to take into account how
many rooms you want to end up with, and for what
you will use them. How much land would you like?
Several or more acres? A large garden or a small
garden? Or just a terrace or courtyard? Would you
like to be surrounded by land even if it is not yours?

Finally, you must ask yourself whether you have
enough time and above all patience to undertake a
full-scale renovation – and it is important to answer
this honestly. You will need to have a certain amount
of fortitude to withstand all the setbacks and
frustrations that almost always arise.

in tune with the old

There is no doubt that an empathy with old houses is like having a sense of colour or style, or an ear for music. It is either something you are born with or something that you have to try to develop if you are the owner of an old house, or want to be, and not an architect or designer specializing in such things. In many ways it is intuitive, a matter of instinctively knowing which style is appropriate within the framework of a house, and how best to treat the house itself. For those who have the gift it is a natural feeling or skill that comes whenever it is needed. Those who do not possess this natural empathy, but who still love the idea of owning and renovating an old house, will need to learn how best to cultivate the necessary sensitivity.

The first thing to do is to try to educate yourself to be aware of the various styles and periods of house building and understand how they evolved. You can learn to appreciate old construction and proportions and the way different old houses should best be treated, decorated and furnished by really looking at (as opposed to just seeing) every old house you visit, and every stately home, chateau or historic building of whatever size and period that you have a chance to look round. You can also study as many magazine articles and books on the subject as possible, tearing out any magazine features that particularly appeal and filing them for future reference.

left

A fully preserved cobbled floor, such as this in the grand hallway of the Chateau de Gignac in Provence, is a very rare sight indeed. It makes a marvellous contrast to the elegant curves of the Rococo side table, the workmanship of the marble and ormolu candlestick and the wonderful sweep of the bottom two stairs.

what to look for

Basically, the four things that make any old building attractive – whatever its state, lack of services, age or size – are architectural quality, materials, setting and atmosphere. By architectural quality I mean its scale, proportion, detail and general decoration. By materials I mean whether it is clapboard or slate and brick, stone or timber, and how gracefully these materials have weathered. Its setting denotes whether it is rural or urban, which aspect it faces (say south in Europe and America, north in the Antipodes), and how it integrates with the surrounding landscape or street or square. Finally, its atmosphere (or spirit or feeling) is a much more amorphous, intangible thing and can be as bad and disconcerting as good and peaceful. Sometimes troubling atmospheres can be changed for the better by new owners, new treatments, new furnishings. In other cases, however, the atmosphere is so pervasive, such a force to be reckoned with, despite a seductive architectural quality and setting, that it defeats even the most determined and sensitive of renovators. I believe that the secret of any successful renovation is having respect for all four of these points. It is necessary to be as sensitive as possible to the building – through innate ability or dogged application – in order to gauge how many changes can safely be made to enhance, rather than compromise, its original attractions.

left

Painted panelled walls provide an interesting textured background for this disparate collection of furnishings: the old pine chest, 1930s chair upholstered in calfskin, modern steel lamp base and cylindrical flower vase.

far left

This fabulous 18th-century plasterwork in Stoneleigh Abbey, Warwickshire, has been beautifully restored and maintained over the years. Astonishingly, distinguished architectural details can sometimes be found hidden under plaster or dry wall board.

styles & periods

2

Once the euphoria about the purchase of an old house or apartment has dissolved into the practicalities, one of the first things to establish is the quality of any existing alterations, and the necessary level of further renovations. Style, we are always told, is a matter of suitability, suitability, suitability, so it will help to know how styles have evolved down the centuries.

knowing the style

Clearly, a little knowledge of the various building periods, and the main architectural trends that were prevalent in different eras, will be of value in instilling confidence and equipping you to judge better how houses should or should not be treated. Moreover, it can only add to your general sensitivity towards old houses to be shown how various socio-economic and technical developments in different decades led to different styles that, up to the mid-19th century – the age of eclecticism – were emulated with varying degrees of sophistication from the top of the market to the bottom. These styles also travelled from one country to another, merging into each other with varying degrees of success, depending on how well they were interpreted by native builders and craftsmen. Since new styles often appeared in response to fashion crazes and were taken up by the cognoscenti while the older ones continued to be built, styles often overlapped in time, and key features of a new style might be applied to old methods of construction, resulting in transitional forms.

Once you have familiarized yourself with the evolution of styles, it is fascinating not only to do detective work in your current or future house, but also to be able to detect the influences on so many of the public buildings erected over the past two centuries, not to mention most of the private housing built since the 18th century. Many so-called 'revivals' are built in the manner, at least, of the past, with varying degrees of success, although most often including misinterpretations and strange mixtures of styles, particularly houses in various suburbs in the United Kingdom and America, with their false beamed exteriors and gables.

It is not unusual for people to say that they live in, for example, an 'Elizabethan-Georgian' or a 'Queen Anne-Tudor' house without seeing anything anomalous in these terms. Architects for late Victorian and Edwardian industrialists and other moguls were adept at mixing the Gothic or the

Medieval with the Tudor or the Baroque for enormous new country mansions. Many 19th-century apartment buildings on both sides of the Atlantic were called 'Louis Revival' and copied Rococo architecture. New York apartment blocks constructed during the late 19th century and at the turn of the 20th century were, and still are, described as 'Victorian Renaissance', while a multitude of interwar and postwar houses in the United Kingdom are known as 'Tudorbethan'.

It is sometimes hard to determine the exact age of many of the clapboard-sided 'Colonial' houses, emulating the late 17th- and 18th-century originals, that were built in enormous numbers on the East Coast and in the southern states of America from the 19th century to pretty well the present. This style proved enduring popular because it is comparatively easy to reproduce handsomely and to adapt gracefully to modern needs and services. This ease of adaptation has meant that many small American towns and villages have a cohesion and unity that is now lacking in so many older European communities, with their outer rings of mostly unaesthetic contemporary housing detracting from the unexpected harmony and charm of the higgledy-piggledy mix of periods within.

above

The flow of rooms one to another without a connecting corridor indicate that this timber-framed house with its beamed rooms dates from before the 17th century. With research and the help of local records, though, you would be able to date it more accurately.

right

This enfilade of early 18th-century rooms is in the Chateau d'Ansouis in Provence. Lived in by generations of the same family more or less since it was first built, the chateau has been well maintained all along the way, and added to and improved when needed or financially viable.

Year	FRANCE PERIOD/MONARCH	FRANCE STYLE	ITALY STYLE	GERMANY/ AUSTRIA STYLE	BELGIUM/ NETHERLANDS STYLE	SCANDINAVIA STYLE	Year
1500		Gothic	Renaissance	Gothic	Gothic	Gothic	1500
1525	François I (1515–47)	Renaissance					1525
1550	Henri II (1547–59) François II (1559–60)			Renaissance	Renaissance	Renaissance	1550
1575	Charles IX (1560–74) Henri III (1574–89)						1575
	Henri IV (1589–1610)						
1600	Louis XIII (1610–43)		Baroque				1600
1625							1625
1650	LOUIS QUATORZE Louis XIV (1643–1715)	Baroque				Baroque	1650
1675				Baroque	Baroque		1675
1700						Late Baroque	1700
	REGENCE [regency of Duc d'Orléans to Louis XV, 1715–23] LOUIS QUINZE Louis XV (1715–74)	Early Rococo Rococo	Late Baroque			Early Rococo	
1725							1725
			Rococo	Rococo	Rococo	Rococo	
1750							1750
1775	LOUIS SEIZE Louis XVI (1774–93)	Neo-Classical	Neo-Classical			Neo-Classical [Gustavian: Gustav III, 1771–92]	1775
	DIRECTOIRE Directoire (1795–99)			Neo-Classical	Neo-Classical		
1800	EMPIRE Consulat (1799–1804) Napoleon I (1804–15)	Late Neo-Classical [Empire]	Late Neo-Classical [Empire]	Late Neo-Classical [Empire]	Late Neo-Classical [Empire]	Late Neo-Classical [Empire]	1800
	RESTAURATION Louis XVIII (1814–24) Charles X (1824–30) LOUIS PHILIPPE Louis Philippe (1830–48) Napoleon III (President, 1848–52)	Rococo Revival / Neo-Gothic		Biedermeier Neo-Gothic	Biedermeier	Biedermeier	1825
1825							
1850	SECOND EMPIRE Napoleon III (Emperor, 1852–70)	Eclectic	Eclectic	Louis Seize Revival	Eclectic	Eclectic	1850
1875	THIRD REPUBLIC (1870–1940)						1875
1900		Art Nouveau	Art Nouveau [Stile Liberty]	Art Nouveau [Jugendstil]	Art Nouveau	Art Nouveau [Jugendstil] + Arts & Crafts [Larsson]	1900
		Belle Epoque					
1925		Art Deco International	International	International	International	International	1925

chronology of styles & periods

BRITAIN

	PERIOD/MONARCH	STYLE	
1500	**TUDOR**	Gothic	
	Henry VII (1485–1509)		
	Henry VIII (1509–47)		
1525			
1550	Edward VI (1547–53)	Renaissance	
	Mary I (1553–58)		
1575	**ELIZABETHAN**		
	Elizabeth I (1558–1603)		
1600	**JACOBEAN**		
	James I (1603–25)		
1625	**CAROLEAN**	Early Baroque	
	Charles I (1625–49)		
1650	**CROMWELLIAN**		
	Commonwealth (1649–60)		
	RESTORATION	Baroque	
	Charles II (1660–85)		
1675	James II (1685–89)		
	WILLIAM & MARY		
	William and Mary (1689–94)		
	William III (1694–1702)		
1700	**QUEEN ANNE**	Early Neo-Palladian	
	Anne (1702–14)	[Queen Anne]	
	GEORGIAN		
	George I (1714–27)		
1725			
	George II (1727–60)	Neo-Palladian	Slight Rococo inc. Gothick and Chinoiserie
1750			
	George III (1760–1820)	Neo-Classical [Adam style]	Neo-Gothic
1775			
1800		Greek Revival	
	REGENCY	Late Neo-Classical [Regency]	
	[regency of Prince of Wales to George III, 1811–20]		
	George IV (1820–30)		
1825	William IV (1830–37)		
	VICTORIAN	Eclectic	
	Victoria (1837–1901)		
1850		Arts & Crafts	
		Aesthetic Movement	
1875		Art Nouveau	
		Queen Anne Revival	
1900	**EDWARDIAN**		
	Edward VII (1901–10)		
	MODERN		
	George V (1910–36)		
1925	Edward VIII (1936)	Art Deco	Neo-Tudor
	George VI (1936–52)	International	

UNITED STATES

PERIOD	STYLE		
		1500
		1525
		1550
		1575
COLONIAL (1608–1720)	Renaissance [Jacobean]	1600
		1625
		1650
		1675
		1700
GEORGIAN (1720–80s)	Baroque [William & Mary]	
	Early Neo-Palladian [Queen Anne]	1725
	Neo-Palladian	Rococo	1750
	Neo-Classical		1775
FEDERAL (1780s–1810)		
		1800
EMPIRE (1810–20s)	Late Neo-Classical [Empire]	
GREEK REVIVAL (1820s–40s)		
	Neo-Gothic	1825
VICTORIAN (1837–1901)		
	Eclectic	1850
	Arts & Crafts [Mission]	1875
	Colonial Revival	
	Aesthetic Movement	
	Prairie School	Art Nouveau	1900
MODERN (1901 onwards)		
	Art Deco	1925
	International	

dating a building

When a building is described as belonging to this or that period it means that it has the distinct style characteristic of the period when it was built. Up to the end of the 19th century, in what is loosely termed 'the West', a particular period was generally known by the name of a British, French or other European monarch, regency, government or dynasty.

There are also more generalized terms, which are listed in the chart on pages 26–7. Although these styles more or less followed each other chronologically, they also overlapped and influenced each other, and there was considerable cross-fertilization between countries, with accompanying differences of interpretation. Moreover, some of the characteristics of the more generalized styles like Gothic, Baroque, Rococo, Classical/Neo-Classical, recur in different guises and at different times. Since travel was long and communications poor until the early 20th century, early European styles took time to cross the Atlantic, Pacific and Indian Oceans, and so were slightly out of sync, as it were, when they were adopted in their new environments.

Unpretentious buildings – the farmhouses and cottages, and small urban and village houses – were nearly always simpler, 'rougher' versions of the prevailing styles, versions that often went on being built long after the original influence or methods of construction had been superseded by new ones in the more sophisticated centres. Then, too, different generations added on to and altered homes, so that it is fairly rare to know the date of a house within several decades, or to find any house, especially a country house, in its unadulterated original state.

What follows in this chapter is a brief guide to how the various period styles evolved and, as it were, multiplied, as well as to the main characteristics of each period. This should help you in the evaluation of any old house, whatever its geographical location, and should also help you to put different characteristics and features in some sort of context.

left

The Gothic influence –
with pointed arched
windows, stone mullions
and arched stone door
cases – is very apparent in
this Somerset stone house,
which dates back to the
13th century. Having been
built at a time of political
unrest in England, the
house may originally have
been fortified.

the gothic influence

Very early medieval European houses were invariably
fortified because of the perpetual internecine
warring between various tribes and even families.
The lowest floor of most houses of any size was used
for storage or for animals, and access to the living
quarters was provided by steps leading up to the
next level, where the main living area was the hall,
used for both eating and sleeping. Any architectural
style was generally based on ecclesiastical buildings,
so was usually Gothic in character. Windows and
doors tapered to a point, drawing the eye upwards
and, symbolically, towards God. Privacy and
sanitation were minimal, as was furniture. By the
beginning of the 15th century, as land rivalries were
settled and conditions became more peaceful, it was
not so necessary to fortify buildings. The great hall
was still the most important room, often two storeys
high with an open timber roof.

As the century progressed the old central hearths
with a louvre set in the roof for smoke to escape were
replaced by fireplaces set into the wall, and more
rooms were added: first the *solar* or parlour, then, in
the second half of the century, proper bedchambers.
As glass became more plentiful, oriel or projecting
windows were added to the *solar*, the forerunners of
bow and bay windows, although oriels, unlike the
latter, were always on an upper floor. Kitchens were
at first separate buildings, while bathrooms did not
exist, although many large houses, castles and
chateaux had *garderobes* for sanitation; these were
like vertical passageways running down the corners
of a house through the various floors. They were
provided with wooden seats and drained into the
moat or cesspool below. If there were no such
facilities, chamberpots had to suffice.

the renaissance

At much the same time in Italy, however, the period that the Italians called the *quattrocento*, the peaceful conditions started to set the scene for a completely new movement in building and the arts that is still influencing the world in all sorts of ways. This period later became known as the Renaissance – a rebirth of ideas. Just as the great Italian families began to turn their attention to domestic building instead of wanton destruction, to being patrons of the arts instead of marauding landlords, more and more was being discovered about the universe and its workings, and about the Classical past, especially the scale and variety of Classical architecture.

This fascination with the past began to be reflected in new buildings as well as a new depth of scholarship. The most powerful men of the time were often as able scholars as they were soldiers and leaders, and they started to collect antiquities with the same enthusiasm that they showed for commissioning contemporary artists and craftsmen. Painters, sculptors, ceramicists, metalworkers and cabinetmakers started to create items for domestic as well as ecclesiastical settings.

The dome designed for the cathedral in Florence by Filippo Brunelleschi (1377–1446) was hailed as the first great achievement to rival and even surpass

left

This two-storey arcading supported by Corinthian columns is at the Palazzo Ducale in Urbino. It is dated between 1444 and 1482.

right

Built sometime after 1444, this fortress-like building is the Palazzo Medici-Riccardi in Florence.

Ancient Roman architecture. But neither Brunelleschi nor any other architects of the period attempted to reproduce the domestic interiors of Ancient Rome, as they had no means of knowing what the insides of buildings had looked like. No one did, until the well-preserved remains of Pompeii and Herculaneum (buried under volcanic ash in AD79) were excavated in the 18th century, although there were occasional descriptions of Ancient Greek and Roman interiors in the work of various classical writers such as Homer and Pliny the Elder, and in the much-admired and emulated *De Architectura* of Marcus Vitruvius, an architect of the first century BC.

Nevertheless, Brunelleschi's white or pale-blond plastered wall surfaces with their grey stone mouldings and details have become a classic colour scheme that recurs in and out of the history of design. His application of antique motifs such as pediments over doorways laid the foundations for the revival of Classical architecture in Europe and, later, America. It was Brunelleschi, too, who in association with the architect Alberti (who wrote that decoration was necessarily subservient to architecture and that he hated anything that savoured of luxury or profusion – words echoed by the proponents of the Bauhaus School some 420 years later) established certain rules of perspective and proportion. These were based on idealized human proportions, which even today dictate the standards by which we judge a room.

The 16th-century architect Andrea Palladio (1508–80) worked on and perfected these rules to bring the interrelationships of rooms to a rare harmony. Late Renaissance Italians were far in advance of the rest of Europe in their domestic arrangements. Large villas were divided into rooms, each of which had a specific function. This is perfectly normal to us today, of course, but throughout the rest of Europe at that time the idea was almost unknown.

the spread of the renaissance

By the last quarter of the 15th century, Italian artists and craftsmen had started to make their way into France in search of work, especially after the French king Charles VIII, who had come to the throne in 1483, managed to annex most of Italy. France, however, like northern Europe in general, had grown accustomed to the prevailing Gothic style and found it difficult to adapt to the severe Italian sense of proportion and unity. As a compromise, Renaissance motifs were grafted onto late Gothic buildings – with some rather curious results.

In 1515, however, Francis I of France managed to lure Leonardo da Vinci and some of his Italian colleagues to his chateau at Amboise to spread the Italian influence. Fifteen years later he commissioned two Italian painters, Giovanni Battista di Jacopo (also known as Rosso Fiorentino) and Francesco Primaticcio, to create some Renaissance interiors in the Palace of Fontainebleau, with the help of French and Flemish craftsmen. This move not only profoundly affected the whole course of French interior design, but also had a huge influence on England, Germany and Flanders. Interestingly, of all the motifs introduced by the Italians, such as masks, garlands, nymphs, putti or cherubs, scrollwork and strapwork (decorative work resembling interlacing straps), it was the strapwork that was the most admired; it became a standard feature in French chateaux and large private residences, as well as in the great English houses of the Elizabethan and Jacobean periods.

French architects began to visit Italy and returned home filled with enthusiasm for Italian buildings. At the same time, different Italian architectural descriptions and pattern books were being published, although many non-Italian craftsmen, not understanding Classical rules and proportions, still merely overlaid Classical motifs on other decorative themes. This happened particularly in northern France and in Tudor and Elizabethan England. The Renaissance influence, filtered through Flemish interpretations, arrived tardily in Brittany and Normandy, and then in England across the English Channel, firstly because they were further from Italy than most of mainland Europe. However, in England's case, there was the additional reason that Henry VIII's quarrel with the Pope temporarily stopped Italian craftsmen from entering the country. Nevertheless, because Henry had ordered the dissolution of the monasteries in 1536, money that had previously been allocated to ecclesiastical building was diverted to the construction of private houses, in towns and cities as well as in the country, and for the middle classes as well as the aristocracy.

Rich landowners travelling around Europe to gain an idea of the new styles in building brought back pattern books. The subsequent impositions of the Classical style on the traditional asymmetrical English and Normandy manor houses and their interior details resulted in a whole new architectural form (having very little to do with true Renaissance feeling). This can be seen in the numbers of timber-framed, beamed and gabled northern French and Elizabethan houses, both large and small, that are still standing.

Decorative plasterwork and carved oak beams were used for ornamental ceilings; friezes were decorated with heraldic, animal and floral forms learnt from Italian master plasterers; and the characteristic wall treatment of the period was wood panelling or wainscoting. Linenfold panelling of the late 15th and early 16th century gave way to panels that were either elaborately carved or inlaid with different woods, sometimes with Flemish Renaissance motifs.

Windows increased in size all over Europe as the availability and quality of glass improved, although individual panes were still small, often diamond-shaped and framed in lead. The fireplace remained the focal point of the living room, for its decoration as much as its warmth, and although Gothic-inspired in the Tudor period, it often became, in Elizabethan houses, a two-tiered affair with carved columns or caryatids or both, and typical of the Elizabethan interpretation of Renaissance art. In fact, the true Classical architectural style did not reach Britain until the early 17th century. This was after the English architect Inigo Jones, who had spent some years studying and travelling in Italy and France with his patron, the second Earl of Arundel, introduced buildings based on his sketches of antique Roman details; these were Palladio's villas in the Veneto and some of the French Renaissance chateaux based on classical models. The Queen's house at Greenwich, the Whitehall Banqueting House and the Classical terrace housing in Covent Garden were all Jones's works. Jones's Wilton House in Wiltshire, built in collaboration with his nephew for the Earl of Pembroke in the 1650s, is one of the first great English Classical country houses.

Interestingly, today the styles engendered by the Renaissance go by the names of Italianate, Tuscan and even Rural Italian, all denoting a style based on Italian villa architecture of the 15th century and boasting features like square towers, hipped roofs, gables with projecting bracketed eaves and pairs of round-headed windows. These styles are popular in warm climates as far apart as California and Australia, Florida and New Zealand, Texas, South America and South Africa.

above

This detail from an interior staircase in the chateau at Blois, one of the great chateaux of the Loire valley, shows clearly the influence that the Italian Renaissance had on French architecture. The chateau was built for Francis I, a passionate exponent of the Italian Renaissance, by the architect Jacques Sourdeau between 1515 and 1524.

above

Dutch Colonial architecture is specific to the Cape area of South Africa. This house from 1685 shows the distinct Baroque influence reinvented for the South African climate.

right

Built around a courtyard, the Hôtel de Lanzun in Paris was designed by the great French Classical architect Le Vau in the 17th century. The tall windows are particularly elegant, with 18 panes either side of the stone mullions and semi-circular as well as geometric architraves.

european baroque

In much of Europe, before the start of the 17th century, the idea that a room should be comfortable had not held a great deal of sway. But the whole idea of the Baroque age, which was characterized by liberal curves within the Renaissance Classical framework and an extensive use of frescos, moulded ornamental stuccowork, stone figures, inlaid and parquet floors, faux marbles and woods, was to fuse paintings and sculpture, furnishings and architecture into one sumptuous creation. Decoration, furnishing and entertaining became passions.

The Baroque style emerged first in Italy, and Italian decorators and craftsmen travelled all over Europe to fulfil commissions. All the same, glory passes. Italy became divided and overrun, and the design torch passed to France, which consolidated its supremacy so dazzlingly during the reign of the Sun King, Louis XIV, who built the Palace of Versailles, that all other European monarchs turned to France for guidance in matters of design.

Louis was fortunate in that in 1633 Louis XIII, his father, had founded a kind of royal cooperative, the Manufacture Royale des Meubles de la Couronne. His purpose in doing this was to provide furnishings for all the royal residences and to help instigate a national style. In this he was greatly assisted by the middle classes, which helps explain why towns and villages all over France that were built or had expanded during the 17th century had, and still have, a charming harmony.

Among all the magnificence of Versailles, much of the effect depended on the careful directing of the natural light through the countless splendid windows. The ground-floor, full-length 'French' windows, or doors, have been with us ever since. But Louis XIV's influence extended all over Europe in other ways. His Revocation of the Edict of Nantes in 1685 and the persecution of the Huguenots meant that many skilled craftsmen fled to other parts of Europe and even, as early settlers, to America.

britain out of the mainstream

left

Oxburgh Hall, a great 16th-century house in Norfolk, is an excellent example of Britain out of the mainstream of the rest of Europe. The castellation and the wide moat give the house a fortified air. With its massive Elizabethan chimneys and oriel windows, it is quite unlike any, say, French house of similar size and period.

right

A close-up of an extraordinary carving by the 17th-century, Dutch-born English master carver and sculptor Grinling Gibbons. It depicts an interesting mixture of a painter's palette, paints and brushes, together with a collection of navigational equipment. This rare piece has been lovingly preserved.

Britain, meanwhile, was undergoing radical changes both politically and technically, especially in its building techniques. The European Baroque style, with its mainly Dutch and Flemish twist, influenced such skilled architects as John Vanbrugh, who was responsible for the great English Baroque houses of Castle Howard and Blenheim Palace. Plasterwork at this time reached new heights of sophistication, as did woodcarving, particularly in the hands of Grinling Gibbons.

Political changes included the unification of England and Scotland under James I, the execution of Charles I in 1649, and the Puritan era of Cromwell and the Commonwealth. The luxurious Restoration period (from 1660) was ushered in by the return of Charles II, who had been deeply influenced while in exile by the Palace of Versailles and the Louvre, as well as by all things Dutch during his sojourn in Holland. There was also increasing emigration to America, notably by Cavaliers (supporters of Charles I during the English Civil War) to Virginia, by former West Indies plantation owners to the southern states, and by Puritans to the East Coast.

Wildly seesawing though they were, none of these political changes and the consequent changes in style affected British building practices as much as the depletion of timber stocks. Wood had been used freely ever since the Norman invasion of 1066, but felled trees had never been prudently replaced. By the beginning of the 17th century there was deep concern over the ever-diminishing wood supply. Laws were passed to restrict tree felling, bricks and stone were used for construction as much as possible, and coal began to replace logs for fires. This made it easier to conform to the basic precautions against the spread of fire that had come into force in London after the Great Fire of 1666. This was just as well because towns and cities were expanding rapidly, and to cope with it the basic plan of the terrace house was developed in the latter part of the 17th century.

the first american houses

While the British aristocracy was busy building grand houses featuring early elegant variations on Italian Classicism with sophisticated French detailing, the rest of the country was building rather simple houses and cottages that were both a hangover from the late Middle Ages and Elizabethan designs and a result of Cromwell's Puritanism. This workaday style travelled to the East Coast of America with the early settlers, and in translation it became the first American Colonial style, sometimes called Cape Cod.

The 17th-century houses with simple clapboard exteriors and plastered and whitewashed interiors, with dashes of Dutch, German and Scandinavian influences, were of very similar construction to the old Tudor and Elizabethan houses, made better suited to the American climate by the outer layer of clapboard. Well-preserved examples of this style can still be seen in Ipswich, Massachusetts, and Sandwich, Cape Cod, as can the old 'salt boxes' dotting the Connecticut coast. (Salt boxes are houses with one side of the roof swooping much lower than the other to protect against the harsh New England winter.) However, the mixture of French Huguenot refugees, displaced plantation owners from the West Indies, English Cavaliers fleeing Cromwell's strictures and younger sons of the British aristocracy sent to build new lives in a new country made a more lavish mark with their newly built houses in Virginia and the Carolinas and the emerging southern states. The Spanish and French type of Baroque, meanwhile, made itself felt in Louisiana and the South West.

When the Dutch king William of Orange married Mary of England, and subsequently shared the British throne with her (1689–1702), the Dutch version of Baroque became a stronger influence on the British, who had started to build in the Dutch manner after the return of Charles II, and on the more prosperous American settlers. The elaborate forms of the high European Baroque were thinned down to simplified and domesticated lines enriched by the blue-and-white porcelains, lacquerwork and silks imported from the East by the newly formed Dutch East India Company.

Bedrooms started to be built off corridors or staircases rather than leading one into another, and parquet and inlays began to be used much more for floors. As the 18th century got well under way and American villages grew into towns, then into cities, at an astonishing rate, there was a vigorous search for more elegance and comfort. At first this was epitomized by the graceful Queen Anne style (1702–14), an extension and refining of William & Mary architecture that lasted much longer in America than in Britain. Exquisite 'Queen Anne' period houses are often called 'Wren' houses in America after one of Britain's greatest architects, Sir Christopher Wren (1632–1723), although these charming mainly brick buildings with a middle pediment, a pedimented doorway and a hipped roof are not Wren creations. They were simply built in the time of Wren by clever American craftsmen and architects who had studied his marvellously detailed pattern books; Wren himself was far too busy designing Saint Paul's Cathedral in London, Trinity College Library in Cambridge and Greenwich Hospital, to name but a few of his celebrated buildings.

above

The 18th century in America was a glorious time for house building. By then, America was developing its own style of architecture, although it took advantage of mainly British pattern books for its architectural detailing. This house, which was built around 1725, is a good example of domestic architecture of the period.

right

Furniture, furnishings and decoration are as true to period as possible in this late 17th-century American room, right down to the pieces of blue-and-white porcelain.

english palladianism

Although Inigo Jones had introduced the ideas of Andrea Palladio to Britain in the mid-17th century, ideas that even at that time were a century old, they were not adopted to any great extent until the 1720s. However, in 1715 Lord Burlington brought home with him a whole series of original Palladio drawings from Italy. He reproduced them, and their public circulation resulted in several faithful copies of villas designed for the Italian sun being built in the damp English countryside. 'Perfectly contrived for the coolness agreeable in Italy, but killing in the North of England,' Lady Mary Wortley Montague wrote to a friend in 1752.

The style did not remain unadulterated Palladio for very long. With the British talent for appropriate assimilation and interesting regurgitation rather than bold originality, the underpinnings of the previously admired French and Dutch Baroque were amalgamated with Classical Palladianism to form English Palladianism, another style as uniquely British as Tudor and Elizabethan.

English Palladianism went on to set the pattern for both grand and smaller houses, as beautiful as any to be seen in mainland Europe, and some extraordinarily elegant houses in America, too. Among grand English houses of this era were such masterpieces of construction as Lord Burlington's Chiswick House and Mereworth Castle in Kent designed by Colen Campbell, both based on Palladio's Villa Rotonda near Vicenza, and Houghton and Holkham Halls in Norfolk. Smaller houses included the gloriously uniform terraces,

left

Chiswick House, which is also known as Burlington House, in west London, was built by Lord Burlington, the great 18th-century expositor of the Neo-Palladian style. Burlington's inspiration for the house came from Palladio's Villa Rotonda near Vicenza.

right

Although these early 19th-century houses in Charleston, South Carolina, are uniquely American in style, it is easy to discern the various Neo-Classical and Greek Revival influences at play. Balconies, porches and loggias such as these are very much an answer to South Carolina's sultry heat, as are the brilliantly white buildings.

crescents and squares designed and built in Bath by John Wood the Elder and his son, John Wood the Younger. These were so universally admired, and the Palladian pattern books so widely distributed, that by the last quarter of the 18th century the components of the style could be copied by literally any speculative builder and the most humble carpenter and bricklayer, and adapted to any budget and plot of land. Hence the rows and rows of gracefully proportioned terraces to be seen in old towns and cities on both sides of the Atlantic – for through the circulation of pattern books, English Palladianism became a strong influence on developing American regional styles under the umbrella title of Early Georgian. Increasingly, prosperous merchants, as well as plantation owners in the southern states, built magnificent mansions for themselves, actually quite unlike anything in England (except for some of the detailing) in new towns and ports around the country as far apart as Newport in Rhode Island, Salem and Boston in Massachusetts, Litchfield in Connecticut, Portsmouth in New Hampshire, Philadelphia in Pennsylvania, Annapolis in Maryland, Williamsburg in Virginia, Charleston in South Carolina, Savannah in Georgia, and Natchez and New Orleans in Louisiana.

One should not forget that the Classical style was made even more popular than it might have been by the European and particularly aristocratic British habit of sending young men off on the Grand Tour – a cultural perambulation around the foremost cities and towns of Europe. Junior scions of noble families returned not only imbued with the Classical and Renaissance ideals but also bearing numerous trophies – paintings, sculpture, furniture, jewellery, fabrics and rugs. They then had the money to employ the best architects and craftsmen to build, alter and furnish their own or their families' new houses to evoke what they had seen on their travels.

left

Designed by Joseph Collins
Wells, Roseland Cottage in
Woodstock, Connecticut, is
very much in the *cottage orné*
genre, an off-shoot of the
late 18th-century/early 19th-
century Picturesque style.
With its vertical clapboard,
the house is more uniquely
American in appearance
than those of a similar style
and period in Britain.

below left

A Gothic house in
Gloucestershire designed
by William Halfpenny.
The Gothic style was partly
the result of an excess of
Classicism, in the same way
as Neo-Classicism was the
answer to an excess of the
extravagances of the Rococo.

right

The Rococo style was never
as popular in Britain as it was
in the rest of Europe, which
makes this fine example of
English Rococo plasterwork
something of a rarity.

rococo

Just as English Palladianism was developing in
Britain and America, the elegantly informal Rococo
movement, crystallized in France during the French
Régence period (1715–1723), was sweeping most of
the rest of Europe. The style was a strong reaction
against the formality and grandeur of the late Louis
XIV's court at Versailles, which had become gloomy
and far from sunny by the end of the Sun King's
reign. By the time of Louis's death much of the
court had drifted towards the more pleasurable
atmosphere created by the Duc d'Orléans, who
became Regent to Louis XIV's grandson, Louis XV.
The Duc was a connoisseur of architecture and
decoration, and the Rococo style was all lightness
and sparkle, colour and fantasy, with endless
mirrors and candles, gossamer-fine plasterwork,
pale painted panelling and curves.

The style reached its apotheosis in the first half
of the reign of Louis XV (1723–74), who was 'only
really happy', as his mistress Madame de
Pompadour is reported to have said, 'when he had a
heap of architectural designs spread out before him'.
Houses and furniture of the period are often known
as Louis Quinze. Just as English Palladianism was
perfectly suited to the grand houses of the more
sober British aristocracy as well as the prosperous
new American merchants and plantation owners,
so the French Rococo brilliantly reflected the
sophistication of Parisian life. With the usual help
of pattern books and peripatetic architects and
craftsmen, the movement quickly spread to Italy,
Spain, Portugal, Austria, Hungary, Poland,
Bohemia, Russia, the Netherlands, Scandinavia,
and, most of all, Germany.

The Rococo flourished in Germany. With the
country still divided into principalities, there was
intense rivalry, each prince trying to outdo the

other. Unfortunately, this style of immense complication needed a sure touch, and in less experienced hands it became effusive and vulgar. As early as 1737 the architect and critic Jacques-François Blondel lamented the 'jumble of shells, dragons, reeds, palm trees and plants that is the sum total of decoration nowadays', but the movement lingered on in most of Europe well into the 1770s and was resurrected vigorously in America in the late 19th century, in urban architecture as well as furnishings.

In Britain the Rococo had rather less impact on building styles than the Baroque, although it did have some influence on furniture and furnishings. Although there were two interesting offshoots of the fanciful look – the Gothick (with an ironic 'k') and Chinoiserie – this last, like the Rococo movement, was largely confined to furnishings.

Batty Langley's book *Gothic Architecture* (1747) caught many people's imagination, and its ideas were taken up, although what resulted ultimately bore as little resemblance to medieval architecture as Post-Modernist designs did to Palladianism. The style remained sporadically fashionable, especially in its most exaggerated form, in the early 19th century, with exotic lodges and *cottages ornés* (artfully rustic buildings, often with a thatched roof and roughly hewn columns) in the grounds of country houses, until it was overtaken by the full-scale Gothic Revival of the 1880s. Batty Langley, incidentally, had an enormous influence on American regional architecture as builders and craftsmen diligently copied numerous designs for doors, mantels, windows, cornices, pediments, columns, architraves and panelling straight from another of his pattern books, *The City and Country Builder's and Worker's Treasury of Designs*.

neo-classical

The second half of the 18th century is considered one of the golden ages of architecture. In the mid-1750s the excavations of Herculaneum and Pompeii, with their astounding discoveries of houses and villas with their ancient decoration intact, sparked an even greater interest in and understanding of Classical architecture and decoration.

Le Goût Grec or 'Greek Taste' was the term the French used to describe their own Classical interpretations, which had overtaken the taste for the Rococo. One of the first French architects to practise the new style, Louis-Joseph Le Lorrain, provided drawings for a dining room in the grand Swedish house called Akero, owned by the Swedish ambassador to France, Count Carl Gustave Tessin. The room was so admired by his friends, including King Gustav, that the style took hold in Scandinavia as a whole and became known as Gustavian Style.

Meanwhile, Madame de Pompadour, Louis XV's mistress, had commissioned Jacques Ange Gabriel, Louis XV's court architect, to create a perfect little Classical building for her. All the major rooms of Le Petit Trianon were rectangular and smaller than usual, and Gabriel then proceeded to design a series of such *petits appartements* at Versailles. This started a fashion for smaller rooms and much simpler furniture than was typical of the Rococo style, with tapered, fluted legs. The style became the norm in the next reign, and was known as Louis Seize.

Neo-Classicism was the first truly international style and has come to be accepted as the term to describe the architecture and art of the last four decades of the 18th century and the first part of the 19th century. However, theoretically, the term really denotes more of an attitude towards the architecture of antiquity. It could be said that with the excitement generated by the excavations at Herculaneum and Pompeii, the dispersal of knowledge by the graduates of the Grand Tours, and the more generalized prosperity and easier travel of the time, all the

various European, American and Colonial versions of Classicism started to come together. The result was a simpler, lighter look, although each country still produced its own subtle variations.

Great British architects of the time were Robert Adam, Henry Holland, James Wyatt and William Chambers. Adam was a remarkable innovator and the first British architect to design complete interiors down to the smallest detail, so much so that the term Adam Style has entered the language permanently, denoting Classical forms freely embellished with ornament culled from Ancient Roman domestic decoration. All of them, though, produced splendid houses, and since fashion was the leitmotif of the 18th century, fashionable styles filtered down through all levels of society.

far left

This glorious painted panelling is in the Haga Pavilion in Stockholm, designed around 1790 by J. L. Desprez. As can be seen in this elegant Swedish interior, Neo-Classicism was really the first truly international style, since interpretations around the world were remarkably similar in feel.

above

Robert Adam, the master of Neo-Classical architecture and decoration, designed this splendid interior in Nostell Priory, Yorkshire. The slender plaster panels show the classical ornamentation culled from Ancient Roman decoration. It was not for nothing that Adam was nicknamed 'Bob, the Roman'.

late neo-classical

The Directoire period of Napoleon's Consulate was the interlude between the Neo-Classicism of the Louis Seize period and the somewhat heavier Classical archaeological style of Napoleon's Empire. More fashion than style, it was very similar in feeling and designs to the elegant restraint of the early Neo-Classicism of the preceding Louis Seize period. The often somewhat florid, not to say pompous, Empire style, however, used a great many adaptations of old Hellenic (the French had started to favour the Greek school as opposed to the Adam devotion to Rome) and Egyptian motifs and a good deal more gilt and elaborate plaster mouldings. Both these styles remained popular in Europe and America right up to the 1840s. Interestingly, the devotion to Classicism on the part of the French was more of a moral and intellectual allegiance than an aesthetic one because of Rome's early republicanism.

This was also one of the reasons why post-revolutionary America found the French versions of Neo-Classicism so attractive, turning towards France in a spirit of brotherhood and gratitude for its help against the British in the War of Independence. Having so recently achieved independence, it was appropriate to turn to a different variation of Classicism for inspiration. In fact, Americans never quite got over the English influence, at least as far as architecture. American Empire, with its heavier furniture and lines, and generous use of the American eagle, was really the declining years of the much more elegant Federal period, which, in turn, was loosely based on a unique American synthesis of the Directoire and the Adam style of Neo-Classicism. However, it was the first truly American style, based on Ancient Rome but basically executed in clapboard and white paint.

At the beginning of the 19th century, the French Greek Taste was transmuted into American Greek Revival. This ebullient but gracefully unique American style is epitomized by the White House.

above

The Federal style in America in the late 18th and early 19th centuries was yet another style based on the archeological discoveries of Ancient Greece and Rome. This pillared house, in Lyme, Connecticut, known as Lord House, was built around 1812. New England is full of elegant Federal style houses lining the streets of pleasingly homogeneous small towns and villages, and so often fronted by picket fences, which are usually painted a dazzling white.

right

The exotic Royal Pavilion, in Brighton, East Sussex, was designed for the Prince Regent, after the Hindu style, by John Nash between 1815 and 1822.

early regency

The same emphasis on Greek Classicism, but with different results, was also to be found in Germany and in Britain under the Regency of the then Prince of Wales (later George IV), standing in for his father, the stricken George III, from 1811 to 1820. In cultural terms the Regency period was considerably longer, lasting from the 1780s to 1830. It encompassed such different crazes as Greek Revival Neo-Classicism, at its zenith between 1805 and 1810, particularly in Scotland; the fantasies of the Picturesque style; and the exotica of the Prince Regent's Royal Pavilion at Brighton, based on Hindu architecture.

The Picturesque, or Romantic, style emerged in the late 18th century when nature and fresh ways of looking at it became very fashionable. Drawing rooms were brought down from the first floor, or *piano nobile*, to garden level, and French doors, or windows, opened onto terraces and lawns. In this new style, buildings had to sit as naturally as possible in their settings, and views from windows had to be contrived to their best advantage. Haphazard symmetry began to be preferred to the more severe rectilinear lines of classicism, and buildings whose parts had been added randomly at different periods were felt to be very pleasing. At this time, too, the Gothic style came back into favour both in Europe and in America, greatly reinforced by Sir Walter Scott's popular Waverley novels and his medieval romances, as well as the publication in France of Victor Hugo's *Notre Dame de Paris* (1831), which in its turn led to the French Renaissance Revival of the Louis Philippe period. The mansard roofs and elaborations of the early French Renaissance buildings were emulated in the historicism that filtered through so much of Western architecture in the late 19th century. This post-Renaissance style was also favoured in America for apartment building and mogul housing, so to speak, although the most popular American building style of all remained the Colonial.

into the 20th century

Queen Victoria came to the throne in Britain in 1837 and reigned until 1901. The term Victorian is equally extensive, covering a multitude of different styles that were pervasive over most of the world.

The rapidly burgeoning middle and professional classes demanded new houses, which put enormous pressure on already overcrowded cities. New towns and suburbs sprang up wherever practicable, usually near places of work and stations. Fairly simple Neo-Classical patterns were used for terrace housing and small country houses before the second half of the century, but as time went by they began to be embellished with ostentatious details from a variety of styles. Elaborate ironwork and

woodwork were much favoured in America, Australia and New Zealand. In mainland Europe and America, where the emphasis was on entertaining, rooms opened out into each other, but in Britain, where the preference was for privacy, rooms were generally given separate access.

In America, after the Civil War, the railways spread all over the country, connecting even the most remote regions. Increasingly, in Europe and the Antipodes, and particularly in America, the most successful members of the prosperous, upwardly mobile middle classes joined a swelling upper class. This new rich elite of railroad, industrial, mining and banking magnates pursued the building and furnishing of their new houses with dedicated zeal. The more sumptuous and extravagant the mansion, the greater the success it signalled. Neo-Rococo, Renaissance and Gothic styles were much in favour, as was Scottish Baronial, emulating the old Norman castles.

The century ended, architecturally speaking, with the Arts & Crafts Movement in America and Britain, followed by the Art Nouveau Movement, which in one way or another was fairly universal. The styles were actually the antithesis of each other, the latter a

search for a modern, ahistorical style, the former
a combination of nostalgia for the Rococo and an
obsession with sinuous vegetal and floral elements.

In Britain, Philip Webb's designs for William
Morris's Red House at Bexleyheath, with its exposed
brick fireplaces and unrelieved woodwork, set the
pattern for the classic suburban and country home
of the early 20th century. In America the style, as
practised by Frank Lloyd Wright (1869–1959) and
his peer group who had adopted the American
Prairie School style, was all clean, geometric lines.

At the turn of the century, a third style emerged
on both sides of the Atlantic. Dubbed Queen Anne
Revival, it closely resembled its early 18th-century
namesake. It produced comfortable red brick country
and suburban houses, all light paint and light filled,
with elements of Arts & Crafts and Art Nouveau.

modernism

In America, Frank Lloyd-Wright had a strong influence on the early pioneers of Modernism, even though his original Prairie School houses had been developed for conditions quite unlike anything in Europe. His philosophy was that a house should develop from within, and as far back as the 1890s he had been using sheeted windows whose patterns dominated the interiors as well as visually 'breaking up' the outside landscape as viewed from the interior. Wright's large suburban villas with their boldly exposed internal brickwork, prominent fireplaces and chimney breasts, and combinations of contrasting textures must have seemed revolutionary at the time. Likewise his low, spreading houses of the early 1900s, with their open-plan interiors and, even more so, the group of houses he designed in Pasadena, California, during the 1920s with concrete interior walls left untreated.

In Holland the Dutch architect Gerrit Rietveld (1888–1964), an admirer of Wright, and a leading member of a young group of architects, designers and artists called *De Stijl* (the style) after an avant-garde magazine of the same name, was determined to create a style that had no link with the past. His architectural masterpiece was the Schroder house in Utrecht, finished in 1924. With its clean-cut appearance, devoid of mouldings, and its metal-framed windows in continuous strips running up to the ceiling, it was a template for those formulating the new International style.

Wright's ideas also inspired the German architect Walter Gropius (1883–1969), who had worked for a short time in Peter Behren's architectural practice alongside Ludwig Mies van der Rohe and Le Corbusier. From producing a programme for using standardized parts for the mass production of small houses, Gropius progressed to reorganizing the Weimar Arts & Crafts School for the Grand Duke of Saxe-Weimar. This led to the founding of the Bauhaus (meaning House of Building) School in

far left

This 1930s interior is in the
Highpoint Flats in Highgate,
London. It was designed by
the architect Lubetkin, a
well-known Modernist of
the time. Although the
building is getting on in
years, it still manages to look
remarkably fresh.

right

Rather different in mood
from the house pictured on
page 48, this Frank Lloyd
Wright design is also in
Chicago, Illinois. It is a good
example of Wright's Prairie
School period and way in
advance of its time.

1919, and the training of a new generation of
teachers who would in turn preach the need for
a general streamlining of surfaces and details
throughout Europe. The School was hugely
important in establishing the relationship between
design and industrial techniques. Mies van der Rohe
(1886–1969) was a director of the Bauhaus from
1930. After World War I, steel and glass became
acceptable for domestic use, and he used these
materials with a severely restrained colour palette
to illustrate his famous dictum 'Less is more'.

Mies's German Pavilion at the Barcelona
International Exhibition (1929) established a
prototype for the best of the future International

Style. Beautiful proportions, sumptuous materials
such as grey glass, green marble and travertine were
contrasted with steel columns wrapped in chrome,
and two reflecting pools in the courtyard were lined
with black glass.

The School was closed by the Nazis in 1933, and
Gropius and other pioneers of the International
Style, including Marcel Breuer (1902–81), moved
temporarily to Britain, taking their new ideas with
them. Mies van der Rohe emigrated to America in
1937, followed by Gropius and Breuer, who had not
found Britain that hospitable to them or their ideas.
In America they found the reverse, and they became
prophets for many architects all over the world.

art deco & beyond

The other major design movement of the early 20th century was Art Deco, which was just as much the antithesis of Modernism as Art Nouveau was of Arts & Crafts. The movement, called after the Exposition des Arts Décoratifs in Paris in 1925 (although it actually started much earlier), was more an interior style than an architectural movement. It used a grouping of individual elements such as furniture, fabrics, ceramics and glass against backgrounds with Classical details like fluted columns, stylized baskets of fruit and inset bas-relief patterns on Classical or allegorical themes. However, it became very popular as a building style in the 1920s in America, particularly in New York, California and Florida. It emphasized opulence as much as functionalism, with engraved glass, gold plating, gold and cream tiles, elaborate metalwork, friezes, contrasting woods and black-and-white granite exteriors.

Although Modernism and Art Deco were both powerful movements, the 19th-century revivalism and nostalgia for past styles could not be damped down so easily. This can be seen in many city and town suburbs all over the Western world, not to mention the ribbon development between cities and towns. Popular revivals that took place during the 1920s and 1930s were Neo-Georgian and Tudorbethan in Britain, Neo-Colonialism in America, Neo-Rococo in mainland Europe, and 'Tuscan' in the Antipodes. World War II interrupted most of this development, particularly in Europe, but there was a resumption of much of the same in the 1950s, despite the resurgence of some brave new architects and designers and the mood of postwar optimism.

left

This splendid Art Deco hall is in Eltham Palace, London, a stunning combination of Art Deco and Medieval styles.

above

This 1930s London cinema, is decorated in the Egyptian Revival style. The popularity of Egyptian themes was due to the archaeological research that was carried out on the pyramids at the time.

understanding your building

3

It is helpful to know the architectural styles that originally influenced your home. However, knowledge of building and furniture styles is one thing; understanding how to apply it is quite another. A mix of research and creativity is your best guarantee of success.

getting to know your building

Before starting any renovation it is essential to have some idea of the building's age, and the various phases of its development (if any), quite apart from its general condition. Any work undertaken on a really old house should be based not just on an efficient strategy for repairs, revival and, maybe, additions, but also on a good understanding of the various periods and styles. This means a sympathy with their respective ingredients, decoration, materials and details – this is crucial if you hope to be faithful to the spirit of the place, if not the original furnishings.

It should also be interesting to try to find out as much as possible about the building's history. This is comparatively easy if you happen to own a distinguished house, of whatever period, especially if it is recognizably by a well-known architect and its progress down the years has been well documented. Research becomes much more exacting with an ordinary house, particularly if various bits have been added or altered over the decades or even centuries.

The grander the house, the easier it is to date it from points of style typical of certain periods, and the more details are likely to exist about its provenance. Smaller, simpler, generic or vernacular old houses are often quite hard to date within a hundred years or so, at least from the clues available in the building itself, although a great deal might be discovered in local and public record offices (see doing the detective paperwork, pages 58–9) and any local history societies. If no such societies exist, it often helps to start one, for there will probably be a number of like-minded people in the area, who, once galvanized, will enthusiastically join you in the painstaking assemblage of local facts and details.

how to date a building

Even if they do not call on the services of an
architect known to be sensitive to old buildings,
most buyers will nearly always have to employ a
reputable surveyor to analyse and assess a building
before purchase, as this is generally necessary in
most countries for a mortgage, quite apart from
a plan of action. Once contracts have been
exchanged, a full structural survey with accurate
plans and sections will be immensely useful,
especially if you have to apply for various
permissions. A good architect or surveyor, or a
specialist builder, with training and experience in
old local buildings should be able to date a house
fairly accurately, but this is not always possible,
particularly at the beginning of a purchase, or in
another country from your own. So it is useful to
have some degree of knowledge about how to date
buildings. In any case, it is exciting – and often

moving – gradually to uncover details of previous
existence and work; to do at least some of the
detective work yourself.

The four main ways of dating an old building are
as follows, and it is more than likely that you will
end up using all of these methods:
- Assessing the proportions of a house and the
  style of its various elements (windows, doors,
  fanlights, staircases, fireplaces, floors and
  architectural details as well as the general
  building style, its roof type and chimneys);
- Assessing its building materials, building
  techniques and structural details;
- Assessing any archaeological evidence;
- Researching written records, local records,
  plans and pictures, and finding out as much as
  you can about a house from long-time residents
  of the area.

As you go about your assessment, note the
proportions and shapes of windows and window
openings, as well as how many panes of glass there
are; the pitch of the roof and its construction, the
details of the eaves, the type and number of
chimneys; all the various fireplaces and
mantelpieces; internal mouldings and details; the
kinds of internal roof vaulting; and what sort of
panelling there is, if any.

Examine, if you can, the shape, size, condition
and type of building materials such as tiles, timbers,
stones and bricks, and the ways in which they are
fixed and joined together. Different periods had
different methods of construction, so sometimes
the actual size of old bricks can offer a good clue
to a building's age – the size of a brick laid flat has
changed very little since medieval times.

If you are trying to discover archaeological
evidence, you will need to analyse the plans of the
building and the way it was developed as well as
scouring the property for signs of overlay. Is it
possible, for example, that one part of the building

is earlier and another part later? Does an existing wall cover an earlier one? Is the house built on top of much earlier foundations?

Written records, hearsay, word of mouth, church-related documents, parish registers, old maps and drawings, and deeds connected with large estates are all worth pursuing for clues (see below). One thing generally does lead to another.

What you must do is remain objective. It is too easy to form a preconception, then to bend the evidence a little, because it seems so 'right'. The date stone engraved on the façade might have been moved from another building, or it commemorates a birth rather than the date of the house. Old drawings might have been romanticized; a building might be listed as 'being of special architectural or historical interest' and given a probable date, but those 'dates' may have been arrived at by assessing the outside only.

Even when there are definite stylistic clues, remember that builders in one part of a country might have got the message long after the original fashion had waned in another, and some styles reemerge, notably the Gothic and the Classical. There are such faithful copies of some periods, right down to the old materials and methods, that it is hard to believe a house is a facsimile. My own feeling is that one should not get too hung up about the exact age and provenance of a building. You love it or you don't. You feel a certain empathy with that elusive spirit of a house for no logical reason. And very, very few of them remain genuine examples of this or that period without some sort of addition or reconstruction acquired over the years.

doing the detective paperwork

Unless you know that the house is distinguished, start your research at the local records office and the diocesan registry. The former should have deeds, sales catalogues, wills and probate inventories, large-scale maps, estate maps, tithe maps, copies of

right

A literally scooped-out room with the upper floor removed in a Normandy house. The removal of the ceiling reveals much of the construction of the building as well as providing a soaring and dramatic space to furnish with a charming eclecticism.

Glebe Terriers (lists of property owned by each church in the area), and rate or tax records, all of which should help in your efforts to date the building. You can also see by the maps the dates when a building did not yet exist. If it does not have the church-related documents, go to the diocesan registry. Glebe Terriers often contain useful details like drawings of the rectory or vicarage and any other buildings owned by the church. Tithe maps show all the buildings and land on which fixed charges were made after the original tithes were abolished and are particularly useful for the accompanying tithe apportionment, which gives the names of owners and occupiers at that date.

The local planning authority will tell you if the building is listed as being of special architectural or historic interest. If it is, there should be a brief description and a probable date available.

If the house is really old, consult, in the United Kingdom, the Manorial Court Rolls. The system of recording the tenancies of copy-holders predates ordinary leasehold agreements and such evidence may go right back to medieval times. Be prepared, however, to have to understand archaic Latin, or at least take along someone who does.

Studying Tax Returns in a records office can be quite rewarding, since there were numerous levies or excise duties imposed on domestic buildings in different periods.

Consult local history societies. If you find that there are none in your area, think of starting one.

If the house is known to be architecturally distinguished, look in the drawings collection of the Royal Institute of British Architects, or similar institutions that exist in other countries. Also research the statutory lists – anything built before 1850 should be listed. In the United Kingdom the National Monuments Record in Swindon, Wiltshire, is useful. Other countries will have much the same kind of records.

windows & shutters

Unless you have a very large, strictly Classical house (in which case it will probably be the columns or pediments or colonnades or even statues that first attract the eye), it is the windows that will give the outside of a house its character. And it is these very same windows, if crassly 'modernized' or insensitively replaced, that will ruin the look of a façade. So if you want to be sensitive to your old house, the maintenance and, if necessary, replacement of windows must be done sensitively and well and out of an informed choice. This means that it is necessary to know a little about the history of windows and their design. Fortunately, it is often possible to renew sills and parts of frames and to carry out other improvements and repairs to bring the old windows virtually up to new standards at a much lower cost than total replacement.

There are two common types of window. The first are casements, more or less the first kind of glazed windows that could be opened, which came into general use in the 16th century. The second are double-hung or sliding sashes, which date from the late 17th century.

casement windows

Most European countries, including Italy where the great Classical tradition took root most strongly, embraced casement windows and shutters, whatever the shape of the frame. In Britain they generally opened outwards, while in mainland Europe they nearly always opened inwards.

In medieval Europe most houses had little or no glass in their windows. In the 14th century glass was extremely rare in domestic buildings. By the 15th century there was a little more glass to be had, but most windows were still protected with shutters or, occasionally, parchment or draughty wooden or reed lattices. If you look at any house façades in European Renaissance paintings, you will probably see a popular window of the time – a cruciform shape with four-lights (that is, the openings between the mullions, or stone or timber uprights, of a window). The top two lights, which could not be opened, often had minute leaded-diamond panes, while the two major lights on each side of the mullion had just shutters or sometimes pieces of trellis. This cruciform shape was an elongated version – taller than it was wide – of the mullion and transom (the horizontal stone or timber member dividing window lights) windows, a design that was seen all over Europe for centuries.

left

Although this is a typical Gothic window with vertical and horizontal stone mullions and leaded panes, it would have been rare for a house in the 14th and 15th centuries to have had glass in its windows.

below left

A late Victorian *oeil de boeuf* window, translated literally as 'bull's eye'. The building dates from 1898.

above right

This splendid many-paned and, one might say, many-styled window in a Victorian house in London's Chelsea was designed by the well-known architect of the time Richard Norman Shaw between 1875 and 1877, a period of great eclecticism. Note the wide band of pargeting, or decorative plasterwork, at its base, and the heavy cornice above.

far right

This window is part of an elegant Federation style Australian house and is a variation on the traditional sash window.

Although in grander late 15th-century houses windows had glass, the panes were removable so that the owner could take them away with him if he wished and fit them into the windows of other houses that he owned. A great many window openings of the time were horizontal and divided into narrow lights with stone or timber mullions. But because glass was still so rare, most regular houses still had shuttered windows with diagonally set mullions in a wooden frame and no glass. The diamond pane more or less predominated until the second half of the 16th century, when the occasional rectangular leaded light was fitted.

Early leaded panes are now very rare and if you come across any, be sure that you nurture them and treat them with great respect. Glass of the period was very thin and often varied in thickness from one part of the pane to the other. Panes were small because glass had to be cut from a blown circular disc that was seldom more than just over one metre (just under four feet) in diameter. This is known as 'crown' glass. Sometimes, more expensively, the glass was blown in the shape of a muff-shaped cylinder (hence the term 'muff' glass), which would be slit and opened out. Panes cut from the circular disc often bear a 'bull's-eye' mark from where they were broken off their metal holder, but both types

have pleasurable subtleties of texture, colour and imperfections that catch the light in a way that modern glass cannot emulate.

Wooden glazing bars began to appear in the late 17th century, about the same time as the sash window. Even so, lead glazing continued to be used for very much longer than is generally supposed. From the late 17th century, too, casement windows were set into flat frames with mullions, and occasionally transoms, with no conspicuous mouldings on the outside. Early glazing bars were broad and flat, sometimes made in one piece, but after the William & Mary and Queen Anne periods

above

These tall sash windows date from the early 19th century. The thin glazing bars give the window added elegance.

above right

The original external wooden shutters frame this heavily decorated window.

far right

Simple, two-part internal shutters at this 12-pane Georgian window mean that privacy can be maintained without the need for any curtains.

in Britain and America, and in the rest of Europe as the 18th century wore on, bars became slimmer, so if wooden casement windows have a rather thin glazing bar they will be late 18th- or 19th-century. Casement windows, sometimes with arched frames, with only one (or occasionally two) horizontal glazing bars and a simple dividing timber were introduced in Queen Victoria's reign as a standard replacement for original lead glazing in earlier 16th-, 17th- and early 18th-century buildings. Huge numbers of old vernacular buildings that would originally have had leaded windows have such 19th-century replacements.

double-hung sash windows

Double-hung sash windows are believed to have originated in the Netherlands and to have been used large and with some abandon on the fairly small gabled Dutch frontages. After his return from Holland in the 1660s, Charles II introduced them to Britain, where they were used more sparingly but to good effect. By the end of the century they were being used for almost all better-class buildings.

These sashes were divided into panes with rebated or recessed glazing bars. In the early days of sashes there might have been any number of panes between 12 and 40; glass was still valuable, and, as with casement windows, had to be cut from comparatively small discs or muff-shaped cylinders. Originally the moving sash was held up by pegs or metal pins pushed into holes in the frame, but by the second half of the 18th century most double-hung sashes were hung on cords and weights at top and bottom and had 8, 12 or 16 panes until the end of the 19th century, although the 4-pane sash was introduced in the 1830s.

The squareish 16-pane sash, where the panes are only slightly taller than they are wide, was used charmingly in late 18th- and early 19th-century cottages, village houses and farmhouses, while grander town houses, manors, rectories, Greek Revival houses and so on had the rectangular 8- or (more elegant) 12-pane version, which remains one of the most graceful windows imaginable. Interestingly, a form of sliding sash was introduced in the early 18th century to suit the horizontal shape of converted mullioned window openings. This was a double-hung sash turned on its side without the pulleys and weights and has remained a popular alternative to casement windows for cottages and other old rural buildings.

exceptions

Of course, there are exceptions with frame shapes and glazing as there are with everything. There are sash windows with semi-circular or arched tops to an upper light, and sash windows with Gothic arches and interlaced glazing bars, both dating from the early 19th century. There are round-headed rustic Italian shapes, grouped in twos and threes, and there are *oeil de boeuf*, or bull's-eye, windows and French doors, or windows (both first used in the Palace of Versailles). In the last part of

the 19th century, bay windows and *aediculae* windows came into use. An *aedicula* in this case was a long window framed with two columns, an entablature and a pediment, often with French doors and a balcony, designed to look like a miniature shrine. A version of this, usually without the columns and entablature, is seen on the first floor of town houses throughout France. There are also many mid-Victorian windows that sport marginal glazing bars with stained glass.

Triple-light 'Venetian' or 'Palladian' windows, with a taller arched or pedimented light in the middle, were originally an Italian Renaissance idea but were used first for early 18th-century English and American Palladian designs and then much more in the mid- to late 18th century. They can be inserted quite handsomely into a wider window opening in a Georgian or otherwise Classical house. Bow windows are often misunderstood. They were used for late 18th- or early 19th-century cottages and terrace houses, but more often for shops in the English Regency period.

shutters

From very early on, shutters in various shapes and sizes were used, often as much for security and for withstanding harsh weather conditions as for filtering or screening the sun. Outer shutters were and still are common in mainland Europe and America (in America nowadays, alas, sometimes as flimsy fakes rather than the real thing). Most European houses keep them solidly traditional and, although they are generally flung open in the early morning and early evening to let in some cool fresh air, for the most part they are closed, at least against the hot midday sun, at night and during any absence. Most British period houses used panelled interior rather than exterior versions. Louvre-slatted shutters came into fashion for Regency and early Victorian villas and continue to be used extensively in different formations in many countries, particularly in America and the Antipodes.

interior & exterior doors

Doors consist of two parts: the surround or door frame and the door itself. In the average 16th- and early 17th-century house, outer doors were more often than not made from vertical oak boards and these were nailed to ledges or to a second skin of other boards run horizontally. Any decoration took the form of diamond lozenges and sometimes arcaded panels. When the Renaissance influence began to spread through Europe during the latter half of the 17th century, most doors became panelled, commonly with two panels trimmed with bolection mouldings (mouldings that stand proud of the framing) and divided by a lock rail. Grander houses sometimes had eight or ten panels; however, for the most part, smaller farmhouses, village houses and cottages continued to have vertical oak boards for their doors.

Interior doors during the latter part of the 17th century were surprisingly uniform in whatever region or country, with heavy bolection mouldings, friezes, entablatures, and Baroque details like broken, swan-necked and scrolled pediments. Both exterior and interior doorways, whether of stone or timber, were often adorned with cartouches, swags of fruit and flowers, shells or masks. A favourite was the large semi-circular bonnet, lined with a strong plaster shell resting on sturdy console brackets.

Door frames became less ornate in Europe in the early 18th century, and adapted the simple Classical arrangement of pilasters and pediments that lasted until the early 19th century, except in Britain, where wooden door frames were banned as a fire hazard in 1774. For a century thereafter British door frames had to be made of some fireproof material such as stone or Coade stone (an artificial stone).

Throughout the 18th century most modest houses had six-panelled front doors with simple small convex, ovolo or ogee mouldings. At the end of the century and the beginning of the 19th, however, there was a significant change in that the bottom

left

These inviting French doors lead the way into a bright Provençal interior, complete with polished terracotta tiles and stencilled wall.

below left

A somewhat hybrid door and fanlight with a 19th-century arched stone surround. In the latter part of the century, the upper panels of doors were often glazed in this way, sometimes with small, stained-glass panes.

far right

Internal glazed doors were mostly a 19th-century innovation to enhance the light in inner rooms and connecting areas. This door is attached to a glazed screen wall as well, which gives a sense of airiness to the space.

two panels would often be set flush with the frame and trimmed with some fine reeding or a couple of lines of flush bead moulding with the idea of more easily shedding mud and water if they were kicked up. When bolection mouldings went out of fashion for interior doors, they were replaced with simple architraves consisting of one or more flat fascia bands enclosed by similar ovolo or ogee mouldings to those used at the front. Typical early 19th-century interior door frames in more expensive houses would consist of a reeded architrave with corner blocks and roundels. Four-panelled pine doors with splayed bolection mouldings and a white china knob would suggest the second half of the 19th century or later.

By 1840 four-panelled front doors were the norm, and letterboxes made their first appearance. By the 1860s many doorways were recessed into the façade to give more shelter, and larger houses often had full porticos. By the turn of the century front doors were getting more and more ornate: upper panels were often glazed or small panes of glass with intricate glazing designs were used in combination with stained-glass lights. After 1900, front doors sometimes had a solid panel subdivided vertically and surmounted by six small panes of glass. Inner doors began to be made of unpainted yew or ash as well as the universal pine. Ledged and boarded doors continued to be used in farmhouses and other smaller rural buildings, as they still are today.

If it seems that some of your internal doors are original, it is a good idea to substitute the replacements with others of at least the correct pattern (although old doors are not always hard to come by). If the house has a variety of different doors from different periods, you have a problem. Most interior designers would say that it is preferable for all internal doors to be the same, yet if the door belongs to a period addition you might want to keep the whole look cohesive. In this case it is really a matter of taste and sensitivity.

fanlights

Semi-circular fanlights (so named because of their radiating glazing bars and fanlike shape) first appeared over doors in the early 18th century, during the Queen Anne period. They were decorated with delicate lead, iron or wood tracery, as were the new – and more ubiquitous – rectangular or transom lights. In the early 19th century, Regency fanlights (as opposed to transom lights) were distinguished from their 18th-century predecessors by having a flatter curve.

When plate glass was developed in the 1840s, large plain fanlights without tracery became standard until the 1870s. During the Edwardian era and the Queen Anne Revival, fanlights and margin lights (side glass panels) became extremely eclectic, with many variations of detail as well as inset panes of stained, patterned and engraved glass.

staircases & balustrades

One must always bear in mind that fashion-conscious former generations had much the same urge to strip out old features and introduce new ones as our own generation, at least until recently. Indeed, staircases and their appendages were often removed to be replaced by something grander (and not necessarily better) than the house itself. Early medieval houses had either winding stone or brick newel (spiral) staircases rising in a turret or in the thickness of the walls, or a straight flight of exterior steps running up an outside wall that sometimes had a wood canopy or pentice (a roof with post, pillar or pier supports used to cover outside staircases). These still exist in many old European village and rural houses.

In the 15th century, houses kept to the stone or brick newel stairs but added a variation made of timber, rising around a central pole or 'mast newel'. Right up to the 17th century, when framed timber staircases and open-well formations were developed, the staircases in most town houses, small manors and farmhouses were squeezed in wherever builders could find a space for them, which often turned out to be the recess behind the hearth projection, or winding up around a central chimney. Poorer houses frequently had merely a ladder.

The Elizabethans invented the open-well staircase, which continued to be built up to the 18th century. Early versions had closed strings, which means the treads were housed in the strings or main framing members forming the sides of a staircase (in an open-string version the shape of the stairs is cut out and the treads rest on the string; wall string means the main framing member is fixed to the wall). They also had heavy turned balusters, short flights of oak stairs, a fairly minimal well and newel posts, with ornamental finials like slightly flattened ball shapes.

By the 17th century, grand houses had all sorts of carved newel posts, with balusters cut in a rectilinear version of a column. Lesser houses had splat

above

These barleysugar-twist balusters form one of the first mahogany staircases to be built in London, in 1726. This wall-string staircase has the main framing member fixed to the panelled wall.

left

This sinuous staircase, with a gleaming steel horizontal balustrade and a contrasting wooden hand rail, was designed and installed in 1937 in a now listed and newly refurbished house.

right

This dramatically spiralling staircase,with scrolled brackets decorating the open-string treads, is in the Theatre Museum, Amsterdam. Note the splendid plasterwork decoration of the walls.

balusters, or flat boards fretted out to show the same idea in silhouette. Hand rails became broad, flat and slightly moulded at the edges as the years passed by, and the influence of the Italian Renaissance resulted in massive turned and vase-shaped balusters.

Late 17th- and early 18th-century staircases might have barleysugar-twist balusters and scrolled brackets decorating an open string, or vase-shaped balusters, or columns with sweeping hand rails on top. Large houses sometimes had an open-well staircase with a central bottom flight of stairs that divided into two flights on either side. An alternative was a big full-width balustraded landing to the hall with matching flights descending at either end, with quarter-landings and further flights. Smaller houses often had shorter flights to a small landing, where the staircase would branch right or left. By the mid-18th century, most smaller houses had these dog-leg stairs, although closed-string staircases were still built in rural houses, or boxed-in staircases with a combination of straight steps and winders, sometimes with a door at top or bottom. Grander houses still favoured the open-well style, and turned balusters became even more elegant and inventive, often combining several patterns.

Cantilevered stone staircases started to be installed in many countries in the middle of the 18th century during the Neo-Classical period, with cast- or wrought-iron balustrades. Later, the staircases in houses that were not quite so grand became simpler, with thin, square balusters and plain mahogany hand rails, finishing in a final curve on top of a newel post set into a curled, round bottom step.

As with other elements of a house, owners and builders did not always use contemporary styles, so it is not uncommon to see Gothic or late Medieval, Elizabethan or early 18th-century staircase forms in houses of quite different periods. However, the basic methods of framing a staircase have changed very little over the past 300 years.

fireplaces

Apart from the comfort and charm of the fire itself, fireplaces are invariably the natural focal point of a room, decoratively and architecturally. Mantelpieces from the 18th century onwards are comparatively easy to rip out and replace, which explains why few original mantels (or mantelpieces or fireplace surrounds) remain in situ. New owners often think that a change – or removal – of a mantel will update a room. Others remove them in order to sell them, while some may want to make the fireplace more of a statement and so change what might have been the original fireplace for another. Finally, far too many old mantels or mantelpieces were ripped out and chimneys blocked when they were thought to be unnecessary adjuncts to central heating. When new occupants put back the mantelpieces, though not necessarily unblocking the flues, they often chose surrounds of the wrong period and proportion or poor reproductions. Since they are so strong a focal point, the more sensitive owner will recognize immediately when the fireplace surround is wrong – whether it is wrongly proportioned or totally out of keeping with the period or the mood of the room.

Wall hearths with a proper flue and conventional chimney did not really make much of an appearance until the 14th century, although there were a few in existence in the 12th century. By the end of the 15th century, large open fireplaces with big bevelled lintels, flush to the wall, were to be found in most dwellings. In the 16th century fireplaces in grander houses often had stone lintels formed into a four-centred arch, while more modest buildings were content with a massive oak beam. Large open, inglenook fireplaces with built-in seats appeared at this time. Early 17th-century fireplaces often had massive two-tiered Renaissance-inspired mantels with a characteristic mixture of Classical mouldings and Gothic decoration. As panelling became more popular, fireplace surrounds echoed the features with bolection mouldings but rarely a chimney

shelf. It was more usual to have a panel above the fire in which a painting could be fitted or on which a painter could execute a scene.

In the early 18th century, when Classicism or Palladianism was all the rage, Classical surrounds with caryatids, and Classical heads and terms (pedestals tapering towards the base and usually supporting a bust or pedestals merging at the top into a sculpted human, mythological or animal

above left

The stone fireplace at Falling Water, Pennsylvania, designed by Frank Lloyd Wright, takes up practically one wall and includes a seat.

above

Large, open inglenook fireplaces made their first appearance in the latter part of the 17th century.

left

This enviable fireplace with a marble surround makes a strong focal point placed between the windows.

right

This tall and handsome ceramic-faced Scandinavian stove provides quite another kind of fireplace feature.

figure) appeared. These were followed by Rococo themes for the frieze with decorative slips of marble fitted inside the timber architrave of the surround, partly as decoration, partly as a practical barrier to separate the timber joinery from the fire. These were followed in turn by smaller Neo-Classical mantels in the Adam manner with plain pilasters, *paterae* (flat, round ornaments like rosettes) and swags of corn and ribbon; the reeded architraves with corner roundels of the early 19th century; or marble slabs with incised decoration ending in a Greek key pattern or anthemion (a motif based on the honeysuckle flower and leaf in Greek and Roman Classical architecture), capped with marble shelves. Sometimes the surround consisted of three plain pieces of marble with corner block and roundels.

Later on in the 19th century, mantels became heavier and more decorated. Overmantel mirrors made an appearance, and decorative tiles surrounded hoop-shaped register grates (so-called because they had a register plate to fit the fireplace and often had coded registration marks that included a date). Most houses built between the mid-19th century and the turn of the 20th will have at least one original fireplace, and it is not hard to find abandoned register grates. By 1900 there were as many wooden mantels as marble, including wooden overmantels with shelves for ornaments as well as mirrors. Art Nouveau mantels were a splendid canvas, so to speak, for all the vegetal designs. In Frank Lloyd Wright's Prairie houses, the fireplace and chimney often took up most of one wall and reached to the ceiling.

Arts & Crafts fireplaces tended to hark back to the medieval period, with their large open hearths, and at the beginning of the 20th century many very grand fireplaces were built with inglenooks or built-in seating. Mantels designed from the 1920s to the 1950s were usually much smaller, and tiled in rather unappealing stepped forms, although there were some glamorous Bauhaus and Art Deco designs.

roofs

Obviously, roofs protect a building, so keeping them in good repair is fundamental. Basically they consist of the carcassing structure, which can be inspected from the inside of the roof space, and the tiled covering, which should be inspected both inside and out.

Old roofs normally fit into one of three main categories. The curving cruck-supported roof is distinguished by its through purlins (square section timbers running lengthwise) and a ridge pole bridging from one structure to the next. The single-rafter roof has crown posts to carry the load of a collar purlin; these posts were jointed into the tie beams of heavier trussed rafters, constructed at intervals along the roof. The double roof, probably the most common, is identified by the double arrangement of principal trusses carrying common rafters that rest upon purlins.

However, there are numerous variations, including the M-shaped roof with twin gables and the gambrel roof finishing in a small gable at the ridge. In America, rather confusingly, gambrel describes a double-sloped roof, like the 18th-century mansard roof (named after the great 17th-century French Classical architect François Mansart), with a steep lower slope and flatter, shorter upper portion. This type of roof was used mainly on town houses.

I have outlined the technical construction of the main roof types because you can often tell more about the date of a house from peering into the roof space than from most other construction details, that is, of course, once you know a little about them. A good surveyor, architect or builder specializing in old houses will generally find a trip to the roof space enlightening.

As long as the insulation and heating in a building have been made as efficient as possible, exposed roof beams are not merely feasible but also beautiful to behold.

left

A curving cruck-supported double roof in an old house in Somerset. Note the through purlins (the square section timbers running lengthwise) and the ridge poles bridging from one structure to the next.

above right

This fraternity house at the University of Georgia in Athens has a classic Victorian cast-iron porch. Its elegant columns and decorative screened arches and balustrades, as well as the overhang, make it impressively ornamental.

below right

Like so many rural porches built in 18th- and early 19th-century England, this Doric-columned porch was classically inspired, although, interestingly, the architrave is not Classical in style at all.

porches

The word porch means very different things on either side of the Atlantic. In America the porch is a venerable institution, a way of life even, all year round in benign climates and throughout the summer elsewhere. It is a sort of hot-weather living room, complete with floors of painted wood or, more grandly, marble, rocking chairs, old sofas, hammocks, cane or wicker furniture and hanging plants. Sometimes they are pillared, even balustraded; sometimes they are screened against the onslaught of flies, midges and mosquitoes, sometimes they are too grand and pillared for screening to be suitable. There are countless variations. Basic porch architecture is derived from a mixture of the Classical and Spanish and French colonial domestic architecture of the Southern States. It is the American version of the Indian, East and West Indian, Southern European and Antipodean veranda.

In Europe the term takes in the minimal bracket-and-slab-type sheltering hoods that often add a dash of distinction (as well as shelter) to the façades of cottages and small houses; the charming early 19th-century delicate timber or iron trellis affairs with curved copper or lead roofs; and noble Classical porticoes, closed porches, and bays with a room or rooms above.

Most small European porches are inclined to be a little frail and will often require extensive repairs. Exceptions are the sturdy little stone structures with pitched slate roofs found on the west coasts of France and England, Wales, Northern England, Scotland and Ireland, or the brick varieties of the late 19th century and turn of the 20th century. But it is important if you have, say, a classically inspired porch, to take care with repairs, and confine yourself to repairs rather than changes, even if you think that the Classical orders have been wildly misunderstood. They probably have been. Still, unless a Classical porch is really hideous, it is best to leave well alone and to copy mouldings and other parts that need to be replaced, painting them tenderly, rather than filling in the dentils and so on, even if you are sure the porch is considerably later than the house. Lots of people have added porches to porchless houses over the years and they look very pretty. On the other hand, Victorian and turn-of-the-20th-century porches with stained-glass side windows, while fine in context, are not so good when added to otherwise beautiful 18th-century houses. So, if you are thinking of replacing a totally rotting edifice, or adding a porch, do make sure that the architectural style and materials of the original building, and, most particularly the feeling of the place, are respected.

Larger porches and porticoes are often prone to faults, depending on their age and what weight they carry. Big pillared structures with a room, or rooms, on top may need entirely new foundations. If that is the case, they might need propping up and the columns removed until the foundation work has been completed.

panelling or wainscoting

In the latter half of the 15th century, possibly to try to alleviate draughts and bitter winter cold in rooms heated only by fireplaces, builders started to line walls with vertical boards, roughly lapped together. Slowly the process became more refined and proper panelling, or wainscoting as it was called, began to be used with horizontal rails and vertical stiles and muntins (framing pieces between panels). At first the panels were carved in the linenfold fashion popular at the time. In the 16th century wainscoting was used more and more but plainly. Panels were quite small and square to fit in with the maximum width of the most convenient oak boards that could be bought in bulk, and were framed with simple mouldings.

By the 17th century wainscoting had become much more elaborate as a result of the Renaissance details now available from pattern books published in northern Europe. In grander houses fluted pilasters, sometimes with Corinthian or Ionic capitals, were installed to divide up wall areas, along with elaborate friezes carved with Gothic floral trails,

vine leaves and heraldic beasts, and Italianate motifs of flat ribbon designs. As alternatives there were inlays, diamond lozenges, carved 'nail head' decoration (not nail heads at all but small pyramid shapes, repeated as a band), and arcaded panels like the kind often seen on 17th-century court cupboards. In the middle of the century, bolection mouldings came to be used in conjunction with taller raised or fielded panels and dados defined by horizontal panels divided from the wainscoted walls by a chair rail.

In the very early 18th century, panelling became simpler again, with small ovolo mouldings, and this remained so until the fashion gave way to Rococo or Neo-Classical plasterwork punctuated by skirting, or base boards, chair rails and frieze rails.

In the 19th century panelling was reintroduced, mostly as the result of a passion for the Gothic, Medieval or Tudor revivals. It was again reintroduced at the turn of the 20th century, but generally finished about two-thirds up the wall and was topped with a shelf for ornaments.

above

A detail of exotically carved polished oak panelling in a house in the Lake District, designed between 1897 and 1900 by the well-known architect of the time M. H. Baillie Scott.

below left

A close-up of magnificently worked painted Rococo plasterwork in an 18th-century chateau in Provence. It shows several of the motifs – curves, wreaths and shells – that were greatly favoured during the decorative French early Rococo period.

right

The horizontal tongue-and-groove panelling on this Australian farmhouse is a delightful feature. Careful paintwork has ensured that the detail of the carpentry has not been obscured.

mouldings, plasterwork & columns

Our ancestors had a penchant for decorative internal details from the earliest days. Wood mouldings of various shapes and sizes were used for architraves, door and window and fireplace surrounds, chair rails, skirtings or base boards, panelling, painting and mirrors. Cornices, coves, friezes, borders and ceiling decorations were cast from plaster. Columns, used prodigiously in Classical and Neo-Classical architecture, were upright, circular and usually tapering members consisting of a base, shaft and capital, and were decorated and proportioned according to one of the accepted Classical modes: Doric, Tuscan, Ionic, Corinthian or Composite. The first four were described by Vitruvius, whose writings influenced the Renaissance architects many centuries later. Composite was a later Roman mixture of Ionic and Corinthian. The simplest was the Tuscan, supposed to be derived from Etruscan temples, but the Doric is probably the earliest. The Greek versions have no base, as on the Parthenon in Athens and the temples at Paestum, near Naples. The Roman versions do.

above

This beautiful 18th-century plasterwork frieze is from Stoneleigh Abbey in Warwickshire. The frieze is partly Rococo in feel, with shells and scrolls enclosing an elegantly moulded Classical grouping.

above left

The reeded base and shaft of an Ionic column, together with a pilaster and decorative plasterwork on the wall above the fireplace.

left

A very grand classically inspired hall, complete with a dentil cornice, chair rail and dado and a series of busts set in decorative plaster niches. The handsome marble floor and marble-topped table are brought into the present day by the chair upholstery.

The Ionic, which originated in Asia Minor in the 6th century BC, was more decorated. The Corinthian – more decorated still – was primarily an Athenian invention of the 5th century BC, but was later developed by the Romans, and it was this version that provided the Renaissance prototype.

Columns were designed to carry an entablature (the upper part of a Classical order consisting of architrave, frieze and cornice) or other loads, unlike pillars, which were free-standing, do not need to be cylindrical, and do not have to conform with any of the Classical orders. Pilasters were shallow piers or rectangular columns, projecting only slightly from a wall, and conformed with the Classical orders.

Mouldings were originally used by the Ancient Greeks for their temples and public buildings, as part of the Classical orders for columns and entablatures, but were as practical as they were decorative. The cornice, for example, the top part of the entablature, covered the join between the roof and the wall and was designed to deflect rainwater. The fillets were used as drip-moulds. Architraves (the lowest of the three main parts of an entablature, but also the moulded frame around a door or window) covered the junction of doors or window spaces with walls.

Although they seem to consist of so many shapes, mouldings were in fact composed of comparatively few and quite straightforward elements that were variations on flat-faced, right-angled fillets and curved quadrants. Flat fillets served as punctuation for the curved quadrants, varying in size in proportion to them and depending upon whether

they were used as supporting or main elements. The quadrants were either concave or convex. The process of undercutting a curve to throw a shadow, thus emphasizing the curve, was called quirking. Various curves were also used in combination with each other to build up different forms. The ovolo moulding was named after the Latin word for egg (hence our 'egg and dart' design), but was really just a flat convex quadrant. The 'cyma reversa' was also, correctly, known as 'ogee'. But 'cyma recta', beloved of the Georgians because it gave a much lighter look than its much-used predecessor, the bolection moulding, was also known as 'ogee', which was wrong, since the cyma recta in no way follows an ogee curve.

The early 19th-century preference was for even lighter mouldings, so 'reeded' mouldings were used, so called because they resembled the long, slim edges of reeds. Fewer reeds gave a chunkier look. Or the shape could be scooped out rather than projecting, in which case it was known as 'cavetto'. Later 19th-century architects and designers favoured cyma reversa. At the turn of the 20th century they returned to the cyma recta and the earlier bolection mouldings.

Most of the really fine plasterwork was commissioned for town houses and grand country houses. Although larger rural houses often had nicely executed cornice and decorative ceiling plasterwork by competent craftsmen following pattern books, most cottages and village houses rarely had anything but a simple cornice or cove. Sadly, plasterwork and wood mouldings have suffered the most from the thoughtless rampaging of modernizers who have removed them in favour of blank walls and featureless ceilings. Although it is quite possible to buy ready-made mouldings, there is not a huge choice in plaster and the fibreglass substitutes do not have quite the same definition. Undoubtedly the best – if most expensive – solution is to employ specialist plasterworkers if you want to replace or restore original details.

floors

It is a truism that the floors of nearly all neglected old buildings will need attention. Floors are of two types: suspended (mainly on upper floors) and solid (ground floors). Most troubles stem from the underpinnings of suspended floors, the joists and beams, which are liable to decay through damp or woodworm. Floors in long-abandoned buildings can be so far gone that they will have to be stripped out and replaced. But mostly they just need repairs and some care. This does not mean levelling out, unless it is structurally essential. Sloping and dipping floors are all part of the charm in an old house.

If the structural elements are covered by a good ceiling, the appearance of any replacements does not really matter, but in early houses most underpinnings of upper floors are displayed in the room below in the form of beams or, in the case of later cottages, plain joists and the underside of the floorboards above. These underpinnings are as important architecturally and aesthetically as the floors themselves, and you should not remove any more than the minimum amount of the original floor framing. If decayed beams or the heavy oak timberplate running along the top of a wall into which the beams are jointed were beautifully carved – as they may well have been – you should try to cut in replacement lengths, jointed so that they can still bear the necessary loads. If you do have to support inadequate joists with structural steel or RSJs (rolled-steel joists), it is most important that the disguising covering, if used, should have enough heft. Disguising timber should be substantial and finished with an adze or a hand plane.

Suspended floors are sometimes to be found at ground level, too: over a cellar or basement perhaps, or joisted over brick piers or sleeper walls. These last are usually 19th or early 20th century, and the later they are, the more likely they are to have ventilators (which have obviously been inadequate if the floor is in a bad state). It is essential that such floors should be kept dry and well ventilated.

solid floors

There are, of course, all kinds of solid floors. Many old cottages, lesser farmhouses and village houses have 'grip' floors of lime and ash, bricks laid in a pattern upon beaten earth or cinders, quarry tiles, clay tiles, flagstones, timber lying directly upon a mortar screed, and even pebbles covering the floors of passages. More expensive houses might have granite slabs, encaustic tiles, terrazzo, limestone, marble, marquetry, and old parquet or inlaid wood.

above

This marble floor, with its grey-and-white chequerboard design, is both smart and hard-wearing.

above left

The scars on the floorboards of an 18th-century mill lend character to the interior.

below left

The stone floors in this renovated hunting lodge have been left untreated for a rustic finish.

Both modest and grand houses would have had polished or scrubbed boards. This latter unpolished, scrubbed look was much used in the 18th century and was achieved by dry-scrubbing the boards with damp sand that had been scattered all over. The sand was then swept up, to be replaced by liberally scattered sweet-smelling herbs, which were firmly brushed in. These in turn were then swept up and the effect was fresh and wholesome.

replacement floors

These depend very much on the age and style of the building and what seems to fit in best aesthetically. I have seen people put down smooth concrete slabs to great effect on the ground floor of old houses, polishing them, roughing them up and buffing them with shoe polish and wax, or sealing and

faux-painting them. And large Mexican, Italian, Spanish and French terracotta tiles always look fairly ageless. However, whether you are laying paving slabs, bricks, flagstones, tiles of any description, or any of the marvellous reclaimed old limestone slabs or other old varieties of stone available today, it is important to keep the gaps between them as narrow as possible, with the mortar, coloured to tone with whatever material has been chosen, kept 1–2mm (⅟₁₆in) below the edges. As long as they are firmly bedded to stop them cracking, there is nothing to stop you using roofing slate or stone for flooring. It is much cheaper than proper slate and flagstone. All paved floors should be washed, scrubbed and polished. The polish will look good and prevent the surface from marking, so if you have a largish house it is definitely worth investing in an electric polisher.

If you are replacing floorboards, the cheapest is tongued and grooved softwood, which can look superb and is perfectly correct in most 18th- and 19th-century houses, but because softwood is butt-jointed, it can shrink and leave gaps if it is not very carefully installed. Softwoods include hemlock, spruce, fir and pine, which should be finished with an oleoresinous sealer, then polished if desired. Alternatively, use a couple of coats of polyurethane. If you can afford oak or elm or American walnut, so much the better. Maple, teak, ebony, iroko, mahogany and Australian ironwood and rosewood look splendid but are more expensive than oak. Better still are wide reclaimed or secondhand oak or elm boards, which have the patina of age. Most early boards were much wider than today's offerings, usually more than 30cm (12in), as well as thicker. A final alternative is to paint old floorboards, having repaired or replaced any disastrously decayed or ruined boards first. The paint will disguise any differences in the wood, and will look good in its own right, whether plain or given a design or border. The important thing is to seal it as well as possible to give it lasting power.

where to start & when to stop

Once enough preliminary knowledge has been assimilated – the age and style of the building more or less decided; knowing what absolutely has to be done structurally; what needs to be restored or repaired and how; what replaced; what altered, what facilities need to be added; what, if anything, could be added on; and, finally, if the services of an architect and/or designer will be needed as well as a builder – it is crunch time. This is a crucial period for both practical and discriminating design decisions that have to be taken before specifications can be written and estimates proffered. It is undoubtedly always best to find out just how much the ideal would cost before calculating the amount of work can actually be afforded; whether it can be done all at once, or in stages, according to urgency; and what can be afforded when. A renovating project, like any large and expensive project, *has* to be planned in advance, in order of priority and stage by stage, even if the work can all be undertaken in one operation. It cannot be approached piecemeal, for that is really the road to disaster – both fiscal and aesthetic.

This does not mean there is no leeway to change your mind, or to take other decisions later if necessary. Being able to play around with ideas, to tweak here and there, and to be ready to compromise are part of any inventive exercise, and anyone who thinks such jobs should be cast in stone is greatly mistaken, whether they be client or contractor. What it does mean is that a firm and logical step-by-step route should be established within which there is reasonable freedom to manoeuvre.

If the job is of any significant size, it is almost certain that some sort of professional services will be needed, in which case much will be taken off the prospective renovator's shoulders. Just make sure they are sensitive professional services, which is best ascertained by word of mouth, or by seeing examples of their previous work.

One danger to be avoided is overkill. It should never be forgotten, especially if a house is more than 100 years old, and more especially still if it is a really old and perhaps rare building, that what you are supposed to be achieving is the revival of the building – the prolonging, and in some cases the saving, of its life. Comforts can be installed, elements can be repaired or restored, space can even be added. What you must guard against at all costs is the destruction of the building's personality, not just its original character but the atmosphere it has attained over decades and perhaps centuries.

Most countries have quite stringent rules and regulations about changes to the exteriors of old houses if they are listed in some way, and to the interiors as well, if they are really distinguished. But the sad thing is that the legislation, redtaped as usual with bureaucracy, is not as sensitive as it could be. Much of it has come too late and the people in charge of applying the legislation are not always in tune with the building or its proposed alterations, and don't have the time to attend to the variations of each individual case. It is hard, given the numbers of old houses, and their unique differences, to see how they could do so, even with the best will in the world and the ability to make instant decisions. Once more, the buck really stops with the renovator and his or her perseverance and sense of suitability.

right

This kitchen in a house in Brighton, East Sussex, marries the old coal range, which was original to the house, with modern appliances and a brand new stove and hood. The white stone floor and plants give the room a clean-cut look.

the methods

How best to preserve or retain that elusive thing, a building's character, is the moral dilemma of renovation, especially if you hope to extend the building or if the structure is so decayed that it really needs to be practically rebuilt. How can you best improve, repair, restore, replace, add to or, as it were, customize the house to your needs, without destroying the charm that first attracted you to it? Or how can you best 'cosmeticize', without having to rebuild, some inappropriate addition that has regrettably been tacked on to the original? Or resurrect a house that you are convinced exists under the 'modernizations' and 'conversions' of previous owners? A house that, as an optimist, you have bought, or are thinking of buying, because of its position and its (putative) possibilities.

There are several schools of thought on the sensitive renovation of old houses, but basically they can be marshalled into three main categories. These are the Reverential, the Innovative and the Cosmetic. This last group involves little spare or immediately available money for renovations, but is still appropriate for those who want to try to rescue or improve a house or apartment, or make it as habitable and interesting as possible on a limited budget.

right

This Art Deco home includes a reverential interior with a staircase, light fitting and furniture that are typical of the period. The streamlined forms and predilection for chrome that characterize Art Deco have a contemporary feel that belie their age.

the reverential

Reverential restorers (with the emphasis on the restoration) are passionate and dedicated purists who identify so much with the past that they refuse to compromise on any detail. They will spend weeks, months even, hunting for just the right replacement bricks or tiles, floorboards or old glass window panes. They will hunt down old staircases and balustrades, old doors of the right period, old drainpipes, old bargeboarding, old mantels, original beams and columns. They will haunt demolition yards, and shamelessly rummage through any contractor's skip standing outside a house of similar age and style. They will chip every inch of rendering off old stone, repoint with exactly the right mixture, have every bit of old broken cornice faithfully replicated with the ancient recipe for the plaster of the time.

In extreme cases reverential restorers will forgo modern comforts: electricity, plumbing, heating, air-conditioning, telephones (cellphones might be permitted, as they are free-floating) in order to live life exactly as it was. And it need hardly be said that they will buy only furniture and find old fabrics of exactly the period or earlier. To be just such a reverential restorer you need to have the money, the time, the resolution and, above all, the patience.

the innovative

There are those who point out, quite correctly, that 19th-century additions were made to Georgian houses, 18th-century additions to 16th- and 17th-century houses, and newly invented improvements installed when they were introduced. Indeed, there are so many houses that have layer upon layer of new styles and ways of thinking that it would be absurd to avoid installing thoroughly contemporary additions when renovating them.

To do anything else might at best be pastiche, or at worst overly subservient to the past, as if the present had nothing to offer. Besides, owners and/or their architects might want to show that they have their own ideas, and that they are proud to contribute them to the structure.

The answer, I think, as far as the fabric of a domestic building is concerned, is that you cannot go very far wrong as long as the materials, the scale and the proportions of the old building are not abused, that the detailing is respected (particularly the windows and doors) and that discretion is exercised. If you can open up a house to the present in the best possible way, and still maintain the feeling of age and mellowness without in any way being ersatz about it, so much the better.

Much depends on the quality of choice, as well as the subtlety of design. So many different building materials and components are available today that did not exist until comparatively recently. But so many of these are unattractive shortcuts, or bear no relation whatsoever to the components of the past, that it is crucial to try to keep the original integrity of the house and keep faith with its elusive spirit in the choice of new additions and ingredients. This may sound a tall order, but it should not be, given the sensitivity that can be gained through learning and properly looking. Also, heating, air-conditioning, and modern plumbing and wiring have done much to transform the way in which interior space can be manipulated.

right

There can be no doubt that this London house is an up-to-the-minute conversion of a classic 19th-century semi. Yet the very large new windows placed discreetly at the rear of the building fit well with the old multi-paned windows above. The kitchen extension and tongue-and-groove decking are sympathetic additions.

far right

The neat glass roof and huge floor-to-ceiling window of the new kitchen extension allow extra light to pour into the room, shown in this internal view. The fittings and furnishings are uncompromisingly modern.

the cosmetic

Cosmeticizing a house lies somewhere between the reverential and the innovative approaches to renovating a house, but the difference is that it costs much less. It is more a matter of compromise, of how to deal with, or rescue, an old and decrepit building with a minimal amount of money. Or it can be trying to improve, say, an addition to an older house that is much less pleasing than the original, one that seems jarringly out of place but is nevertheless in too good condition to warrant tearing down or that you do not have the money to replace. Again, it can be a desire simply to bring

back to some sort of distinction, and as reasonably as possible, a floor, or a room, in an old house that has been modernized within an inch of its life, and seems vexingly out of tune with the rest of the building. It can even be as small a job as trying to add storage space as subtly as possible; or to gain more space overall without losing too much of the old room arrangements.

In the case of a wreck of a house, or an addition or wing, you can, according to your budget, substitute roof tiles and hunt for windows and doors to match those in the original building, or those that should

left

The old formation of window panes has been left in this house so that the façade remains unimpaired, but the internal mouldings, like the skirting, have been removed to create an uninterrupted flow of space. The brick floor, however, is a definite concession to age and looks well with the unbroken plaster walls and chunky stone fireplace.

right

A new sash window, black skirting and modern furniture bring this room well into the 21st century, in spite of the 19th-century stone fireplace and the high ceiling. In fact, these components give the room a great deal of character.

have been in the building. Again, depending on cashflow, you can try to find the right old chimneys, reface the exterior with clapboard or plaster or tiles, or simply repaint and plant fast-growing climbers and roses. You might find, once again, that it is new windows that are really bothersome. If you change them to match the others, so much the better. The right windows give instant gratification. If the worst comes to the worst, you can simply add glazing bars – they will still look better from the outside. A new coat of paint or wallcovering, painting over nasty kitchen cabinets, and a good wood or tiled floor laid over cheap vinyl tiles (or just stripping or painting floorboards, or painting over unattractive tiles, if new wood or good-looking tiles are not feasible) will all make a considerable difference.

More sympathetic old fireplaces could be installed gradually to replace dingy 1950s tiled affairs or similar. Skips, as mentioned before, are excellent hunting grounds. Decades of gunge can be stripped off beams and woodwork. Old baths and basins can be refinished with special paint, or replaced with cleaner, better-looking secondhand sanitaryware. More appropriate banisters or balusters and stair-rails can be introduced to make the stairs more seemly. You could even find authentic period staircases with diligence. If you have handyman skills, building a kind of room within a room is an option. Lining the walls of a room stripped of all character with bookshelves is yet another option. More patience and enthusiasm than money might be the rallying cry here.

The more effort that is made to understand and respond to the requirements of an old or older home and the more thought behind the building, the better will be the end result, whatever the timescale and whatever the budget. It may sound sentimental, but almost every battered old house will improve and find its own harmony if it is given a little intelligent appreciation and careful attention.

4

The growing industrialization

of the last 200 years has drawn

people to the ever-expanding

urban areas. As these, in turn,

have grown, people have been

drawn to the outer city,

otherwise known as the

suburbs. As inner-city space

became more scarce, expensive

but still desirable to dedicated

urban dwellers, developers

turned to vertical buildings

divided into apartments.

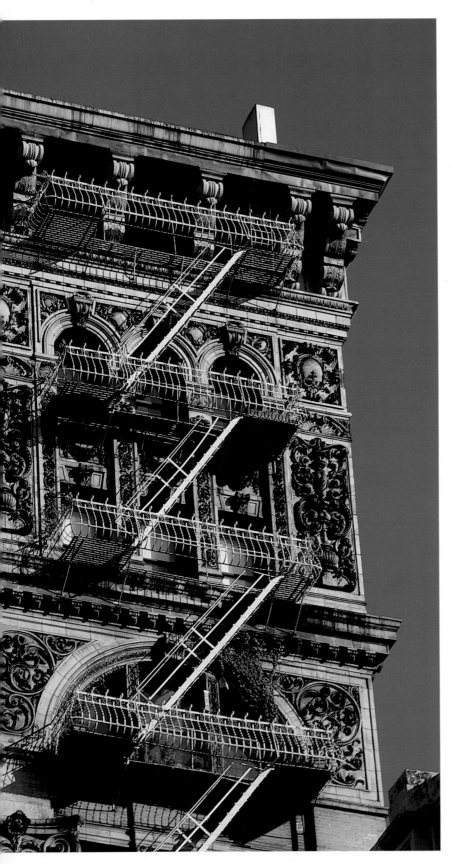

Today most people live in urban areas. This was not always so. In the late 18th century, only about a quarter of the population lived in towns and cities. The aristocracy, landed gentry and richer merchants possessed quite large and splendid town houses, especially in capital cities or seats of government, but their principal and most prized properties were still their country residences. But as industrialization gathered pace in the 19th century, populations swelled, and factories, offices and other places of business sprang up in cities and towns, so houses, and later apartment buildings, were built to meet ever-expanding housing needs. At first, villages and country towns that ringed cities retained their identities as separate communities, but gradually they were absorbed by the creeping development to become outer suburbs, then inner suburbs as the cities oozed on past. Large gardens were eaten into for more houses, and the mews and lanes behind grander terrace and detached houses for servants' quarters and stables became other houses and garages. Country, provincial and coastal towns, whose occupants enjoyed less crowded but nonetheless prosperous conditions, remained fairly contained and to this day possess well-tended streets of covetable and often stunning 17th-, 18th- and 19th-century houses, if not mansions.

After the railways were built and railway stations proliferated, suburban houses started to rise up around or near stations. This gave city workers the choice of living outside cities and towns and commuting back and forth by train, or, later, in cars. In the late 19th century and early 20th, roomy, comfortable houses were built by developers off leafy streets and roads, with matching large, leafy gardens or, in the richer or high-rent areas, quite generous parcels, sometimes a considerable acreage of land. Better-paid middle-class employees with growing families, professional people, captains of industry and financiers, then had the opportunity

left

A highly ornamented, 'reach for the sky' apartment building in downtown New York. Iron fire escapes are a common feature of the city, mounting the front or rear façades of architecturally magnificent dwellings.

right

This clapboard suburban house in its quiet, leafy street has the sort of flexible design that fits into most geographical locations, whatever the climate. Although the interior has probably been altered dramatically by its different owners over the years, the exterior has stayed substantially the same.

far right

These rows of terraced houses in Hebden Bridge, Yorkshire, are typical of 19th-century workers' terraces. Like the suburban house on the right, they have changed little on the outside, but inside they have probably been modernized, the space reorganized and new sanitation and central heating installed.

of living comparatively spacious and rural lives within manageable distances from cities. And not just the better paid. As time wore on, streets of smaller, cheaper houses were erected, still with gardens, to encourage even more people to commute.

In the meantime, congested American cities started to grow upwards to make maximum use of increasingly precious square footage, choked as they were by people who, like the pithy 18th-century English clergyman Sydney Smith, dismissed the country as 'a kind of healthy grave'. Other cities in other countries followed suit. The older apartment

buildings of comparatively modest height and more generous internal dimensions started to become covetable. In the past two decades or so, many families, prompted by deteriorating public services as well as lack of amenities and cultural activities, have moved back into cities, assiduously buying up what were workers' cottages, terrace houses, and former outer-suburb, now inner-suburb, semi-detached houses, as larger inner-city houses have become either steadily more expensive or been converted into equally expensive apartments.

town houses

There are very few really ancient houses extant in most capital cities, at least to live in, but there are a surprising number of well-preserved late 16th-, 17th- and especially 18th-century houses in both European and American smaller cities and towns. Such old town houses as still exist, however, some in large cities but most in smaller towns, are often more intact, more true to their roots so to speak, at least on the outside, than most rural houses of similar age. This is simply because there was little room to expand, or to alter, the original.

On the whole, there was little disciplined urban planning in Europe before the 17th century (except for Ancient Roman towns), and houses grew in a higgledy-piggledy way. From the 16th century, the middle classes (and within them the professional classes) were on the rise and so was house building. However, timber shortages at the beginning of the 17th century caused contractors to switch to stone and brick for as much construction as possible.

By the 18th century most town houses were symmetrical, well proportioned and conforming to a general pattern, so that to a great extent they could be standardized, with added details mostly taken from pattern books. Since architecture did not become a profession until the latter part of the 18th century – great architects before then were either passionate amateurs or extra-skilled and imaginative craftsmen – standardization and pattern books made the task of builders and developers much easier.

Except for the occasional virtual palace built for the very rich and very grand, most large town houses of the time followed much of a formula. The largest and most important rooms, such as the drawing room and library, were normally situated on the first floor, or *piano nobile*, with main bedrooms, dressing rooms, boudoirs and servants' rooms on the second and third or attic floors. Halls, studies, morning rooms and dining rooms were at entrance level, with kitchens and sculleries in the basement. Until the late 19th century, privies, if they were provided, were in an extension to the ground floor, backing into the garden or area from where the waste was collected. Distinctive features of the grander 18th-century Georgian town houses were the semi-circular fanlight above the front door, long windows on the first floor and a parapet to protect the eaves. In American maritime towns like Providence or Nantucket, where many privateers or whaling-fleet owners built their homes, they added wide, balustraded roof decks or widow's walks from which they could look for their returning boats.

Other exceptions to these criteria were usually former country houses absorbed into urban settings as towns expanded. Smaller late 18th- and 19th-century town houses were often various versions of 'through houses' or 'back-to-backs' – working men's houses with formulaic interiors. Through houses had no hall, basement or corridor; the front door would open straight from the street into the living room, with the kitchen behind and two bedrooms above. Back-to-backs were only one room deep but because two houses were divided

above

A terrace of 19th-century brownstones (so named originally because of the colour of the stone in which they were built) in Brooklyn, New York. It is easy to see the changes that successive owners have made to the somewhat formulaic design of their homes. The house on the right has lost the keystones above its front door and windows, and most of the old basement area has been filled in. The windows in both houses are no longer the originals. Nevertheless, the terrace still retains a cohesive look.

above right

A spacious town house in Hudson, New York, with attractive classical details, the fashion for which had reached America from Europe in the 18th century. As was the custom, the large drawing room is situated on the first floor of the house. The original floorboards have been bleached and then whitened.

laterally, it enabled double the number of houses to be built on the same piece of land; for additional space they often had basements and attics.

the practicalities

Whatever the size of the town house you think of buying, decide how you want to live in the space. For example, is it possible to make a house more open-plan for family needs, or to make it seem more spacious, lighter and airier by knocking down non-load-bearing walls, say between halls and living rooms, or between two or more rooms, at the same time retaining and maintaining the exterior? Can you add to the space by making better use of attics and basements, or add to the perceived volume by demolishing whole floors to make a vaulted space? Enhanced light can be achieved by substituting a glass wall, or French doors, or glass bricks at the rear of the house, or by replacing existing non-load-bearing internal walls with etched glass walls.

The given space can be made to look larger and more minimal by sanding and polishing floorboards and leaving them bare, or by getting rid of poor

right

The simple panelling of this urban apartment acts as a foil to the intricate plasterwork above. The antique chandelier adds a touch of glamour to the interior.

left

A sensitively modernized old town house in London with nearly all the original details kept: the panelled internal window shutters, the cornice and floorboards.

right

Although this kitchen-dining area in an old town house in upper New York state has been as sensitively modernized as the London living room on the left, it has a very different, period feel. This is partly due to the older and more eclectic furnishings but also – a more subtle difference – because the original 12-pane windows and narrow dividing muntins, or glazing bars, have been retained.

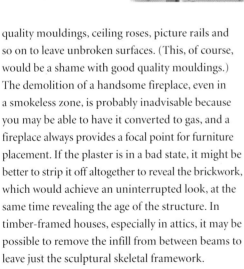

quality mouldings, ceiling roses, picture rails and so on to leave unbroken surfaces. (This, of course, would be a shame with good quality mouldings.) The demolition of a handsome fireplace, even in a smokeless zone, is probably inadvisable because you may be able to have it converted to gas, and a fireplace always provides a focal point for furniture placement. If the plaster is in a bad state, it might be better to strip it off altogether to reveal the brickwork, which would achieve an uninterrupted look, at the same time revealing the age of the structure. In timber-framed houses, especially in attics, it may be possible to remove the infill from between beams to leave just the sculptural skeletal framework.

You may need local planning or listed house permission to make any radical changes, as opposed to sensitive restoration, and you may decide that a period house does not suit your particular lifestyle. If that is the case, concentrate on looking at later 19th-century or earlier 20th-century buildings instead, where no such strictures arise.

Finally, once you have worked out what you want to do and what you are able to do, you will need to know the amount of work that is entailed to preserve the structure or framework. Almost every brick and stone structure in a town or city will have suffered to some degree from pollution, not to mention the havoc caused by heavy traffic and underground railways.

If the brick- or stonework is really dirty, it can be sand-blasted to great effect. Crumbly brick and stone, if not too far gone, will need to be repointed to hold it together better and to weatherproof it. Large cracks caused by movement in the foundations should be treated seriously by competent builders, and cracked and dilapidated stucco should, depending on its state, be stripped down and replaced or at least repaired and painted. Remember, too, that old wiring will probably need to be replaced to accommodate modern safety standards, and you may well want to install security equipment, such as a burglar alarm.

terrace houses

Inigo Jones designed the first blueprint for city terraces, or row houses, as early as 1630. By the 18th century such terraces were built around squares and crescents with communal gardens in front, as well as along regular streets, in cities around the world. They came in various guises, some in gloomy darkish brick, some in pleasant rosy red brick, some stuccoed, some slate, some 'brownstone' as in New York, some creamy-honey stone as in the Georgian city of Bath, some in the distinguished soft grey stone of Paris.

In 1774 the London Building Act was passed, specifying structural dimensions for new houses, divided into four different taxable groups according to the house size and value. This act was intended to avoid any repeat of the Great Fire of 1666, but it also provided a useful formula for other cities and towns, outlining a minimum structural code for foundations, wall thicknesses, and the position of windows for each size of house. The first category was expected to be more than 83sq m (900sq ft), the second 46–83sq m (500–900sq ft), the third 32–46sq m (350–500sq ft) and the fourth up to 32sq m (350sq ft). Unthinkable today, the groups of occupants expected to compose the various categories were also prescribed: nobility for the first, merchants for the second, clerks for the third, and workers and mechanics for the fourth.

This exercise provided a sense of architectural harmony as well as setting certain standards. Nevertheless, terraces had their own pecking order. The centre block often (at least for the first grade) had a grandly pillared and pedimented façade. As was customary for the time, the large reception rooms were on the first floor and had the biggest windows and the most distinguished details, with the smaller reception rooms on the ground floor; the principal, guest and children's bedrooms on the third and fourth floors; the servants' rooms in the attic; and the domestic quarters in the basement. The basement was somewhat shielded and distanced

from the street by railings, and the attic half-concealed by a parapet. Grades two, three and four diminished commensurately in size and detailing.

During the first half of the 19th century, larger, more comfortable houses appeared – these are much easier to adapt for today's needs than the older, smaller versions. Double doors between rooms appeared, to be shut for intimacy or left open for a good through view and a larger space for parties. In large cities an occasional really large terrace house even had a ballroom, which today could be turned into a quite spacious apartment in its own right. French windows led directly on to balconies. Halls, and also back gardens, varied in size and importance depending on the size of the houses.

The last half of the 19th century produced very different terrace structures. Although there were still developments of the Classical style in various countries, it was mainly left behind in favour of revivals like Italian Renaissance and Gothic, even Dutch Baroque – sometimes a mixture of them all.

left

One of the advantages of so many old town houses is the attic. By installing Velux windows or similar, the attic, whatever its shape and form, can be turned into extra living space. In this Victorian terrace house, the attic has been turned into a bedroom and bathroom.

right

The original front and back parlours in this town house have been knocked through to make a more flexible space, with the addition of folding panelled doors to match the internal window shutters. The original floorboards have been retained, but note how they run horizontally rather than in the more usual lengthwise arrangement.

below

White on white on white against glossy, dark-stained floorboards makes for a particularly restful and airy-looking kitchen in a Victorian London terrace. Apart from the floorboards, little remains of the original detailing – the mouldings have been removed to avoid any breaks in the clean lines. The splashbacks are painted MDF, while the worktops are pre-oiled oak.

the practicalities

Given the scarcity of desirable old urban properties, there can hardly be an 18th- or 19th-century terrace house in any city or town in the West or the Antipodes that has not been brought into the 21st century as far as basic contemporary comforts are concerned. The same goes for mansions that have been turned into apartments, sometimes with magnificent results. But for the many that find previous renovations really too basic, it might be best to strip back and start all over again as sympathetically as possible. The heating, for example, may have to be scrapped and re-installed, perhaps with skirting radiators, grids in the floor, or underfloor or in-ceiling methods, which will be more efficient in terms of both heating and space. Some people may wish to swap modern radiators for the old-fashioned variety, although in pre-early 20th-century houses when central heating did not exist, my own feeling is that it would be preferable to make a newly installed system as invisible as possible. As for air conditioning, a thorough renovation should include a central installation to obviate unsightly window units.

A separate bathroom and toilet if they are next to each other could be rolled into one to make a more luxurious space. Adequate storage is always a problem in formulaic terraces, especially if you want to adopt a minimalist approach for which a generous amount of cupboard space is essential. It might be worth considering sacrificing a whole small room on the master bedroom floor, or taking a sliver off the largest bedroom to make a walk-in closet, rather than trying to install adequate closets without ruining mouldings.

Undoubtedly, the biggest challenge for town-house renovators is to make the best of the interiors of small- and medium-sized formulaic terrace houses. This can be done by opening up living areas or by making each house as individual as possible by cosmetic means and with well-chosen colours within a disciplined exterior.

flats & apartments

Although there were occasional 'sets' of rooms in late 18th- and early 19th-century buildings, normally meant specifically for single men, flats and apartments as such were not custom built until later in the 19th century and at the turn of the 20th. There are some very splendid Art Nouveau apartment buildings to be found in much of Europe, the Americas and the Antipodes, as well as Art Deco versions, palatial Victorian Renaissance near-palaces, and Edwardian Dutch and Flemish Baroque mansion blocks. Then there are the first Modernist apartment buildings and the plethora of 1920s, 1930s, 1940s and 1950s American apartments and penthouses first glamorized by Hollywood, as well as the ubiquitous 'studios'. Generally, the older the apartment, the better and more spacious it turns out to be, with room configurations that are easy to change around.

In addition to all the specific apartment buildings with graduated roof levels in every major city, there are the 'conversions', the flats and apartments carved out of old houses with varying degrees of success.

the practicalities

Converted apartments pose by far the greatest challenge to imagination and ingenuity, since the high ceilings and chopped-off mouldings, far from being an asset in a small space, merely turn an otherwise reasonably manageable area into a space that is almost impossible to furnish and decorate with any degree of success.

The best advice in such cases is to do one of two things: either take down the new partition walls and try to bring the bigger space back to its origins (which usually means, at the very least, replacing missing mouldings and maybe doors as well, quite apart from having to create divisions of space with the furnishings); or to lower the ceilings so that rooms, although still small, at least regain better proportions. Another advantage, of course, of

lowered ceilings is that you can install good indirect lighting, which will make a visual difference to the *sense* of space if not the actual square footage

One of the biggest renovating problems in apartments is how to reduce inside and outside noise. Carpets with a good thick underlay, even building an extra layer of wall (sound travels through electrical outlets and this prevents it), are all helpful for minimizing internal sounds. Sympathetic double glazing, that is windows that fit in with the original windows, or at least most of them, help a great deal to reduce outside noise, although they are expensive. Much can be done by utilizing old shutters or purchasing reproduction ones, as well as having lined and interlined curtains. If floorboards are not covered by carpet (and many apartment buildings insist that they are), they should have any gaps filled and be covered generously with rugs.

Storage is a perennial problem in almost every European apartment (but not such a serious problem in America and the Antipodes). Think of utilizing the space around doors and windows without spoiling any existing mouldings or architraves.

left

The plasterwork and mirrored overmantel crowning the marble fireplace is typical of late-19th- and early 20th-century Parisian and New York apartments. Restoring any complicated plasterwork designs is a labour of love. It means searching for skilled craftsmen and finding appropriate old moulds and designs to follow if the original decoration is badly damaged.

right

Making the most of limited space, fitted bookshelves in the dining room surround the wide entrance to the kitchen area of an apartment carved out of a 19th-century town house. Folding doors shut off the kitchen area when necessary. In the kitchen, a stove fits into a former fireplace, and the floor, like the walls and woodwork, is painted white to expand the space visually.

right

A common theme in this home is the juxtaposition of old and new. In the spacious open-plan living area the old beams soften the hard lines of the kitchen where a cooker, ventilated hob and fridge are concealed behind a steel facade.

below right

The elegant Baroque façade of the old palace showing the roof now pierced by a series of regularly spaced skylights.

combining old and new

Prague is one of the few european cities of venerable age and elegance with almost all of its old buildings left intact, apart that is, from superimposed shop fronts, the odd skyscraper lording it over the churches and cathedrals, and ancient Baroque palaces converted into office space. But it is in one of these former palaces that the previous owner decided to turn a two-storey attic under the roof in one of the wings into a thoroughly modern loft apartment. Knowing that it was important to engage an architect who was familiar with both the city and city planners, he engaged the Pra gue-born, London-based and highly talented Eva Jiricna, whose first priority was to let as much light into the space as possible – a priority that meant inserting a series of skylights into the distinctive 17th-century roof line. Predictably, this was not looked upon with favour by the city officials. ▶

right

The entire staircase leading up to the bedroom floor is suspended from the steel mesh attached to the roof. Only the balustrades are attached to the walls. Note the quadrant-shaped reinforced glass landings separating groups of 16 steps, and the contrast of the graceful steel and glass structure against the ancient pine beams.

below

The polished steel balustrade is strung with thinner meshed steel. Although the stair shaft was both high and awkwardly narrow, the design of the staircase visually expands the given space.

location: Prague, Czech Republic

built: 17th century

revived: 1990

Ms Jiricna fought hard, however, and somehow managed to win permission to bathe the space with the light that she craved. Her next battle was to install a staircase in the tall but narrow space formerly taken up by a ladder to the hayloft. The necessary 8m (26ft) was too high for a spiral staircase, and city fire regulations specified a maximum of 16 steps before a compulsory landing space. The only solution was to design a dogleg shape in the cramped shaft. Undeterred, Ms Jiricna worked out the stresses and strains, the thickness and profile, with the help of computer engineer Mathew Wells. Then, because the roof was much sturdier than the walls, she suspended the entire, graceful stainless steel staircase and non-slip toughened glass treads from a steel mesh hooked to the top of the building. Only the balustrades were securely attached to the walls. It is an engineering feat as much as an aesthetic one; a splendid contrast with the medieval timber crucks and the ancient pine beams and joists.

above

This end of the main living space shows the long, custom-made retractable dining table and Charles Eames chairs. They are placed in front of the continuous ledge – useful for extra seating and display space – which runs down the whole of the right-hand side of the room. The new Velux window inserted into the sloping roof line lets in a great deal more light and looks rather good framed by the original old supporting trusses and beams.

right

Since the original sandstone walls were not capable of supporting any significant load, the edgy glass and stainless steel staircase had to be suspended from a steel mesh anchored to the trusses from the top of the loft level all the way down to the first floor. The materials were chosen because of the necessity of bringing as much light as possible into the centre of the building as well as the fact that the lightweight and translucent structure made the space seem much less confined.

right

Two bedrooms with en-suite bathrooms were inserted at the end of the general living space like free-standing cubes. Natural timber floorboards were sited in the centre of the rooms surrounded by the general limestone of the main floor area, and generous storage was provided.

below

The bathroom fixtures – including the bath tub – were all purpose-designed in stainless steel and glass, with all the plumbing and services cleverly concealed by elegant stainless-steel tubes. The bathroom floor, like most of the floors in the apartment, is made of limestone.

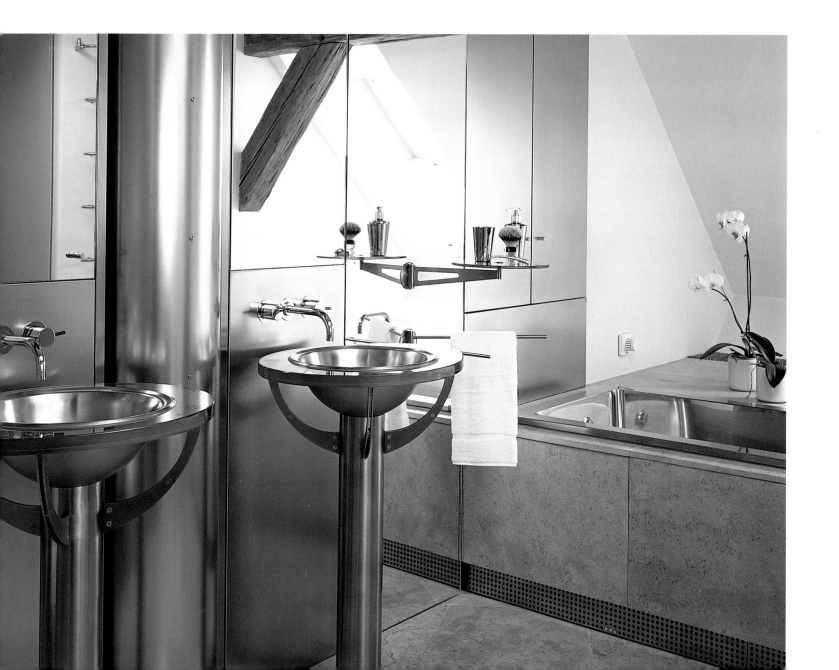

suburban houses

In the latter part of the 19th century, with the proliferation of trains and the first cars, it became fashionable to live as far away from a place of work as was practical. Whereas the early 19th-century population was essentially urban and street-orientated with its balconies, terraces and porches, the Victorian middle classes turned inwards to their families, becoming determined to give them more living space, as well as a garden and a conservatory. This the middle classes were able to do because of lower land values outside the towns and cities, where new spacious but affordable villas and semi-detached houses were being built.

Whole socially homogeneous communities sprang up around train stations, with residents of much the same social order and income pocketed in their various social strata, yet harbouring upwardly mobile aspirations. People tended to keep themselves very much to themselves. Front rooms could be just glimpsed through the lace curtains. Very often the only part of a neighbour's house to be seen was a chink of hall as the front door opened. But oneupmanship was rife, if comparatively subtle.

Things became somewhat friendlier and open with the arrival of the so-called new garden suburbs and a stronger sense of community after the turn of

left

The green-painted shingles and sunbeam porch make this 1930s suburban house in Maine stand apart from other Colonial-style homes of the period. A good carpenter will be able to restore such a unique porch or replicate any shape that seems appropriate to the style of the house.

above right

A spacious, curved Modernist living room in a 1930s suburban house, originally designed to be part of a 300-house development, although only 30 were actually built. The house was altered in the 1950s, and then again in the 1970s, but since the estate was well documented, the current owners were able to put back the original features.

below right

Stained glass for doors and windows and encaustic floor tiles were extremely popular for suburban houses from the late 19th century through to the end of the 1930s.

the century. Some suburban areas started to become more *urbe in rus* than *rus prope urbe*, more town in country than country near town.

In America and the Antipodes, new cities were built in a very different way from the old, with city centres containing offices and factories, galleries, theatres and cinemas, and with most people living out in various strata of suburbs, still graded according to income and status. Suburban houses became quite individual, built in many different styles, and not all were speculatively built. Many people bought plots of land and commissioned architects to design big 'one-off' houses, not necessarily in the latest idiom, unless the Elizabethan, Tudorbethan, Jacobean or Queen Anne Revival was considered a must-have. The Queen Anne Revival became very popular on both sides of the Atlantic because of its combination of Classical and vernacular forms in warm red brick. It was a relaxed and easy style to handle since it could be made as grand or as modest as the purse dictated. Many of these houses, which are now from around 50 to more than 100 years old, have become more inner than outer suburban, or at least much nearer the heart of things than they were originally, and are ripe for conversion to altogether new lives.

As the 20th century rolled on, however, America, Canada, South Africa, the Antipodes and the more enlightened parts of Europe built many interesting new buildings in the Modernist style on suburban plots. These houses are today becoming classics in their own right, with many needing renovations, repairs and updating, a bringing-back-to-life without, it is to be hoped, too much change. Unless such houses are listed, and many are not because of changes made in earlier decades, it is usually possible to install larger kitchens and laundry rooms as well as up-to-date heating, plumbing and wiring without interfering too much with the original design concept.

above

This peaceful view is from the
entrance hall to the arcaded
and balustraded balconies
running around the house.

split personality

'Liberty', or 'Le Style Liberty', was an alternative name for Art Nouveau in
Europe and the Spanish-speaking countries of South America. It was so-called
because Arthur Stewart Liberty, founder of the famous Liberty store in London in the
1870s, was an ardent advocate of the style. This stunningly restored house in Lima,
Peru, is a prime example of the look. In fact, half of the house, the part built in 1909, is
certainly 'a Liberty house', as they call it in the area, but the other part, built three years
later, is actually Victorian Rococo.

   The imposing but split-personality house was first built as a holiday home for a
rich Peruvian family. Alas, the owners lost the house in a poker game, and the grand
collection of rooms lapsed into a sad and dreary state. It was later bought by the
present owners' family but, unfortunately, the purchase coincided with the major
economic downturn of the late 1980s and the house remained a wreck until the Swiss-
Italian architect son-in-law, Umberto Prisco, and his wife Claudia, took over the place
and began a major restoration that has only recently been completed. ▶

location: Lima, Peru

built: 1909–12

revived: 2000–2

above

Most of the double-balconied entrance façade with its distinctive domed roof and graceful columns had to be restored. Note the adobe wall to the right of the stairs.

left

One end of the living room filled with retro 20th-century furniture, mostly serendipitous finds. The double doors to the dining room still have their original stained-glass windows.

left

Now restored, the heavily ornamented wrought-iron balcony in the Liberty style, with the old tiled floor, show that the house is once more at the height of its splendour.

below

Although in contrasting styles, the ornate stained glass and the simple lines of the dining table and chairs work well together. The doors can be opened to the living room, thus doubling the space when required.

left

The master bathroom was
made by Peruvian craftsmen to
the Priscos' exact specifications.
The wooden sink surround
is made of pumaquito wood,
the translucent screen at the
window of calico.

below

The Priscos retained this
internal window with its
original stained glass, although
they felt compelled to replace
some of the Liberty stained glass
in other windows in order to
allow in more natural light.

Before the two-year project could begin, the couple had an enormous struggle with the National Institute for the Protection of National Heritage. The house had been declared a National Monument and the Institute was afraid that the frail structure would collapse during the restoration work.

Because of the differences in construction and style, the work was, according to Umberto Prisco, more like restoring two houses. There was the Liberty part, with its 60cm (2ft) thick adobe walls (a mixture of clay, straw and water, which protects a structure from humidity as well as heat), wooden floors, stained-glass windows and marble stairs. Then there was the 1912 Victorian Rococo part, with its tinted concrete floors and quincha walls. Quincha basically consists of a wooden framework onto which flat pressed bamboo canes are nailed and then covered with plaster – a South American version of the old English lath and plaster. Making quincha walls is an inexpensive pre-Colombian, and therefore, ancient, technique. As with the adobe walls, the porous structure of quincha allows good ventilation. The most difficult aspect of the work was installing modern plumbing and bathrooms – originally water had needed to be drawn from a well in the garden.

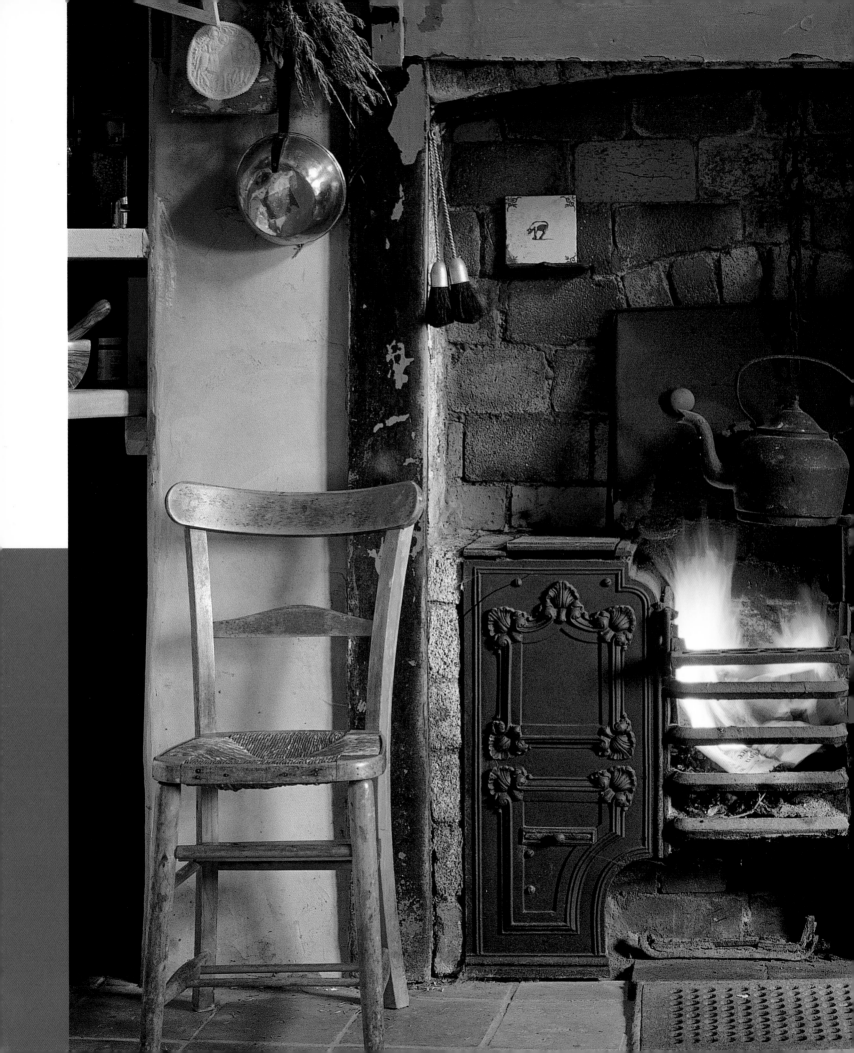

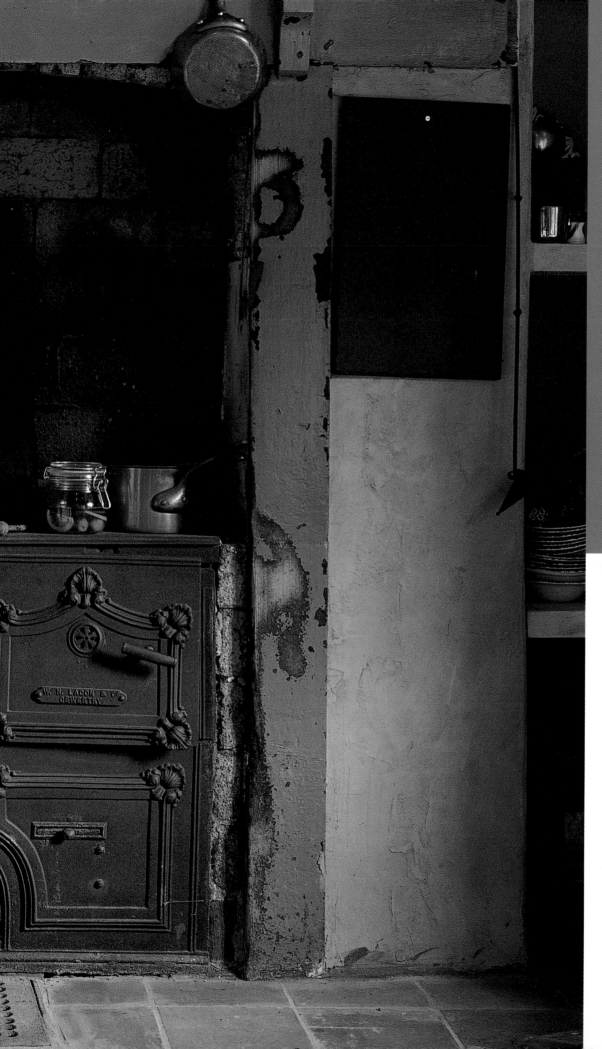

rural houses

5

'The Country life is to be preferred, for there we see the works of God, but in cities little else but the works of men', wrote William Penn, the Quaker and founder of Pennsylvania, in the late 17th century. His thoughts were echoed by William Cowper, the 18th-century British writer, who, a little more succinctly, remarked: 'God made the country and man made the town.'

country living

To live in a properly rural house, not a formal larger country house, but some sort of farmhouse, cottage or village house, in whatever country, is the dream of many – and the achievement of many, too. For technology and agricultural innovations have made many old farm buildings obsolete. Estates have been broken up, farm land has been bought up by ambitious large-scale farmer barons, former country dwellers have moved to towns and cities, and, as a consequence of all these changes, many old houses and cottages have fallen vacant. Alas, since the vacancies have often been of long duration, such houses can sometimes be in a very sorry state of disrepair as well. However, their condition is not so desperate that it is impossible to discern their original structure, building materials and detailing, and very often the kinds of changes, alterations and additions that have been made through the decades.

Generally, apart from some more or less deeply pastoral setting, with an old farmhouse or any rougher country dwelling, you get a proper vernacular house built with local materials in local forms by mostly unsophisticated local builders – with the consequence that it is often quite difficult to date. In the 17th century Gervase Markham, an English agricultural writer, provided plans for a convenient farmhouse that was to include a great hall, a dining parlour with an 'inward closet' for the mistress's use, a stranger's lodging 'within the parlour' and a buttery, kitchen with room for brewing, a dairy and a milkhouse. No mention, interestingly, of any bedrooms, although bedrooms were certainly being added to the general structure by this date, at least in Europe.

left

The simplest possible
construction has been used
for this early American log
cabin in Virginia. In general,
however, the style of houses
in the southern states became
more sophisticated faster than
their East Coast counterparts.
The first 17th-century
American houses with their
clapboard exteriors were
very similar in construction
to Tudor and Elizabethan
houses, with dashes of
influence from the Germans,
Scandinavians and Dutch.

below

These jammed-together
houses, with their distinctive
pantiled roof tops, in Saint
Saturnia, Provence, have
been built wherever space
allowed. Generally, the odd
shapes and apparently small
exteriors of such houses,
which are typical of villages
in the south of France, belie
the space to be found in
their cool interiors.

right

This hillside stone
farmhouse is situated near
the coast in Provence.
It probably dates from the
17th century, but it could
be younger because the
design and materials of
rural houses often changed
very little over the years.
An advantage of a single
house in its own grounds
over a village house is
that there is often room
for expansion.

farmhouses

Whatever your final purchase is, it will almost certainly have been 'improved', rebuilt and added to over the centuries, often with the old dairy, buttery, brewhouse, cowshed and hayloft incorporated into the original living quarters, ready to become a kitchen and dining room, playroom and guest bedroom and bathroom, if there has not been some attempt to ring these changes already. This is not very different, in fact, from the American 'connected' farmhouses, which consist of main house, little house, back house and barn all joined together, and sometimes still added to when new buildings could be afforded, or when later generations had the need. Most British and many European farmhouses started off as either a

primitive 'long house' or, more commonly, a 'hall house', which stemmed directly from the much earlier barnlike structures. To the 'hall houses' were added one or two cross wings. Houses built at the end of the 16th and during the 17th century, and designed as two storeys from the beginning, still conform to the familiar plan of a central block with a single cross wing or two.

If you are lucky, that is to say, if former owners have been sensitive and not built on unsuitable, ugly additions, a farmhouse will have ended up as a long, shambling, picturesque, timber-framed ramble of a building, ready to be adapted yet again to the present. My own clapboard-faced farmhouse in New York

above

The renovation of the interior of this farmhouse in Picardy is entirely sympathetic. The huge open fireplace, heavily beamed ceiling and tiled floors are almost *de rigueur* ingredients in such rural homes.

left

A much more contemporary remodelling, though none the worse for that, of a farmhouse in Tuscany. The kitchen is entirely 21st century, but the thick stone walls and ceiling beams in the living room beyond betray the age of the building. Elongated windows take advantage of the view.

state, which incorporated two barns, took the form of three sides of a square and was equally picturesque. Others might be faced with flint and slate, or be totally built in stone or clay as are so many French farmhouses (known as *mas*), or stone or stuccoed in faded ochre or pink as in Tuscany or Umbria, or stone and plastered mud as in Spain. Many early European farmhouses were fortified with small towers, as were some British ones, particularly in border country between England and Wales or Scotland. Later farms were often built of brick. Sometimes a façade will be lime-washed, sometimes plastered, sometimes left to show the timbers, which is often particularly favoured. But a word of warning here. From the 17th century onwards, most British timber-framed houses were encased in plaster because by then, with the shortage of wood, the timber would probably have been inferior. This is something that all too many would-be restorers are unaware of as they strip away the old covering to reveal less-than-glorious beams beneath. Also, of course, the plaster helped to block the draughts, just as clapboard or white cedar shingles used as cladding in America over timber-framed houses withstood the harshness of the seasons from snow to sun.

the practicalities

The main point to remember in any renovation of a farmhouse is that country ways are simple, in whatever country you may be, and in many respects the simpler and more natural the house, the better. All too often these days the first step in any renovation has to be to peel or strip or rip away all the layers of sad and misguided attempts at modernization that have been made over the past few decades: the hardboard panels over the old banisters and panelled doors; the woodchip paper over the beams; the layers of paint covering original mouldings; the plain sheets of plate glass, or even a 'picture window', where the old mullion or

above

Thick stone walls, the original brick floor, deep reveals to the windows and ceiling beams provide a suitably aged background to an old farmhouse of uncompromising modern furnishings and accessories.

left

This early 18th-century farmhouse in New York state has been faithfully restored with every vestige of previous modernization removed. The painted, wide floorboards, the painted panelling and the bolection-moulding chimneypiece are all American country classics.

right

A 17th-century stone farmhouse in Normandy was bought as a country house and revamped in minimalist style. The white-painted or stripped beams, pale furniture, natural fabrics and sisal matting fit restfully within the early structure, which has mostly been painted white.

casement windows once were; the electric or gas faux-fires instead of the old fireplaces, or worse, no sign of any fireplaces at all.

When all this stripping away has been achieved, and any pests like woodworm or rot eradicated (remember to insist on a written guarantee for this), think first of all how the available space can be reorganized. For example, unless the old kitchen is already large and welcoming, you might consider incorporating any old dairy and other adjuncts into one main space, perhaps turning the old kitchen into a more convenient dining area or room, a spacious and well-equipped laundry or utility room. If there is a fireplace to be uncovered – or even added – so much the better. Other old adjuncts, such as a buttery or tack room, might be turned into a bedroom and bathroom, a small separate apartment for guests or an older family member, a cloakroom or powder room. A hayloft makes an excellent playroom, as does an attic. A barn, too, can be turned into a splendid kitchen-family room or an entertaining or party room, a studio, even a

guest cottage, as can a dovecot or *pigeonnier*. A stable or cowshed attached to the farmhouse can be turned into a home office, study or table-tennis room, even a separate cottage for letting out to holiday-makers.

When all the space has been apportioned or reapportioned, put in new wiring, which will almost certainly be needed. Plan first of all where you want your lighting or power points, and remember that you will also need wiring for security systems, stereo, computers and other electronic equipment, phones and fax machines. New heating and air conditioning can be made almost invisible; if you are going to replace floors or ceilings, this opens up possibilities for sophisticated underfloor or ceiling heat. Of course, it is commendable to restore missing architectural details, to replace old tiles if you can find similar ones, but if that proves difficult and the exterior has been restored or treated sympathetically, there is no need to be slavishly reverential to some part of the past inside. All the same, it would be a shame to iron out any of the quirky vernacular idiosyncrasies that you may uncover.

minimal & rustic

below

Two near-derelict 18th-century cottages and a barn in the Yorkshire countryside were joined together to make a really spacious home with spectacular views. The exposed beams and stone-flagged floors contrast with the minimal but comfortable furnishings to create a space that is crisp-looking with an impressive sense of scale.

This Yorkshire farmhouse was originally two cottages that had not been lived in for 20 years, and a barn that had only ever been inhabited by horses and chickens. But the new owners, absolute beginners at renovation, had great plans. These included joining all the buildings together, transforming the really run-down cottages into a large hall, eat-in kitchen, offices and a dark room with an additional two bedrooms upstairs, and turning the barn into a living and dining room, with a second floor for bedrooms and a bathroom. As dedicated modernists, they didn't want to end up with anything remotely cottagey; they were after large, clean, airy and uncluttered spaces, with the bonus of a rural setting. Their vision and taste, and the help of an empathetic architect, Rodney Heywood, ensured a successful transformation. ▶

location: Yorkshire, England

built: 18th century

revived: 1989

above

Since the owners have dogs, and dogs a seemingly inexhaustable number of hairs to shed, it was felt that leather seating would be the most practical. It also fits in perfectly with the style of the newly created spaces.

right

The handsome maple flooring on the landing was originally the dance floor in a former church hall. The black jug set on the simple table is typical of the deliberately spare decoration chosen for the conversion.

right

The fireplace in the living room, created from the ground floor of the former barn, was designed by the owners' friend Neil Hemingway, and made by a local stonemason.

below

An Aga stove was fitted into the space where the fireplace originally was in one of the former cottages, right under the original lintel.

below
The sofas in the living area were specially designed to an extra large scale by the owner's friend Neil Hemingway. The curtains are made from scrim, which is normally used for lining or for window-cleaning cloths, but they look entirely appropriate as window coverings in this setting.

One of the major setbacks – and let's face it, there are almost always major setbacks in every major building or renovating exercise – was the fact that the old stone from demolished walls, which they had counted on recycling for other areas of the group of buildings, turned out to be too crumbly. This necessitated the purchase of 'new' old stones, which caused a rather dramatic addition to their budget, as did buying a new roof made from Welsh slate, which they felt was more in keeping with the structure than anything else available. Still, they were clever in moving around old components such as door and window lintels to new locations, and fortunate to discover a vast inglenook fireplace behind a considerably less handsome green tiled affair. They also bought a maple dance floor from a former church hall and used it for the floor of the upstairs landing. Although the project ended up costing twice as much and taking twice as long as they had anticipated, they felt that it was, without doubt, well worth it.

cottages

What is the difference between a farmhouse and a cottage? Basically they started out as much the same thing, but cottages stayed smaller, often with just one or two rooms.

Few of the really early European cottages built by lords of the medieval manors, or monasteries, for their poorest tenants have survived because many were so insubstantial that they could be erected or dismantled like tents. In fact, it was a common complaint in the Middle Ages that discontented absconding agricultural workers and peasants would take down their houses and carry off the fabric to set them up again in as distant a place as possible. The late 16th century changed everything. An English statute of 1589, reminiscent of the current American rules on country land parcelling, ordered that no new cottage could be built unless it was surrounded by four acres of land. Nor could more than one family occupy a single dwelling. This was a counsel of perfection that was seldom enforced, but the thought behind the act was to make farmworkers more independent. Enormous numbers of sturdy cottages (including many pairs of cottages) were built during the late 16th century and the 17th, designed for and still sometimes home to rural labourers and their families. (Interestingly, the much earlier Bayeux tapestry shows some equally sturdy French cottages at a time when there was nothing so solid to be seen in Britain.)

Many late 16th- and early 17th-century constructions resulted from the merger of hall and cross wings into a simple rectangular design, a design that was taken to America very early on by the first settlers. But, like farmhouses, much of the delight of these little buildings, on whichever side of the Atlantic they happen to be, lies in the diversity of their compositions – with a haphazard mixture of lean-tos, offshoots, additions and projections – and the way they nestle into their respective landscapes.

left

Painted tongue-and-groove panelling lines both walls and ceiling in this remodelled cottage. No doubt the original walls were quite different in appearance, but the effect now is fresh and inviting, but still with a rural appeal.

right

One room leads into another in this obviously old, wood-framed cottage. Note the change in levels (perhaps indicating a pair of cottages originally) and the exposed framework. Such buildings were constructed on both sides of the Atlantic from the late 16th century onwards, and many have proved sturdy enough to survive much as they were when first built.

left

The beamed and bricked ceiling and terracotta-tiled floor, together with the decorative carving above the door, suggest that this bedroom is part of an old Italian rural dwelling, gently brought into the 21st century with little change.

left

This 1840s Nantucket carriage house had survived rather more than a century with very little done to it in terms of modernization. Then the architect Hugh Newell Jacobsen, admired for his ability to fuse Modernism effortlessly with older references, stepped in to satisfy the new owner's desire to keep the saltbox character while creating a simple, well-proportioned and unapologetically white space. The treatment, right down to the old wide floorboards, fills the house with a luminous light.

right

A sloping beamed cottage ceiling and unadorned whitewashed walls cocoon an intricately shaped, painted iron bed and a gaily decorated chair and chest. The period structure creates the sort of background that makes even the simplest of furnishings look good.

With the 18th century came many more classically oriented farmhouses and cottages. Plans and elevations for the new styles were often included in books on the latest farming techniques, illustrating the remarkable concern for aesthetics that there was at that time. When the new Gothick and Picturesque styles started to make an appearance, architects with no other apparent rural leanings began to conceive of farms and cottages as 'picturesque incidents in a landscaped estate'. A certain John Plaw, author of *Fermes Ornés or Rural Improvements* (1800), wrote that 'farm buildings should be calculated for landscape and picturesque effects' and presented a design for 'a farmyard having the appearance of a monastery'. Even John Loudon, a celebrated and respected gardening and agriculture writer of the time, recommended extravagant Italian and Gothick styles for some of the cottages shown in his massive *Encyclopaedia of Cottage, Farm and Villa Architecture* (1833). This, incidentally, should be standard reading for anyone wanting to study the range of ideas and styles there were for the countryside in the 1840s.

The first part of the 19th century saw the arrival of the charming *cottages ornés*, and of picturesque embellishments like porches and verandas grafted on to much earlier, more primitive buildings. It was the era, too, when the cramped cottage became the epitome of the countryside, of the wholesome way of life, an idea popularized first by the 19th-century Romantics, and then by the leaders of the Arts & Crafts Movement. C. F. Voysey, an influential English Arts & Crafts architect and designer, urged: 'Try the effect of a well-proportioned room with white-washed walls, plain carpet and simple oak furniture and nothing in it but necessary articles of use – and one pure ornament in the form of a simple vase of flowers.' The average agricultural worker or cottager of the time might have smiled wryly at these words, but it was this sort of notion that shaped the way we see cottages now.

village houses

left

One of the many charming things about unsophisticated village houses is that the simpler the renovation, the more appealing the end result. In fact, meticulous detail would almost certainly look out of place. A fairly haphazard and often half cosmetic remodelling, as in this rural kitchen, makes such houses a delight to be in.

However small the mainland European village, it will be a fairly homogeneous honeycomb of rural architectural styles of different periods in every size, with houses apparently glued together as they progress up the hillside or down the narrow streets. British villages will have at least one or two 'big' houses, with one or more old farmhouses whose occupants used to farm surrounding village land. Most of the other buildings will be cottages of different styles and periods, some in pairs, some in pairs converted into one, some semi-detached, some in terraces, with the streets clustered around the village church, pond or green. The big difference in comparison with many European villages is that some British

right

This cobbled and leafy seating area outside a studio room built onto a village house is ideal for relaxation. Outdoor rooms such as this are an accepted extension to interior spaces that can be cool and rather shadowy.

below left

The living rooms of village houses tend to be small and need fairly careful planning. Here, the central sandstone fireplace, built-in bookshelves and checked cotton-lined cupboard doors are a good advertisement for the virtues of simplicity. Note the larger checks of the tiled floor and the sculptural look of the Thonet bentwood rocker.

above

Grey walls, a white trim and
chequerboard floor tiles are
a subtle combination in this
small village house, and
make a restful background
for the furnishings.

above right

The white-painted wide
floorboards, moulding-free
walls and pale-painted
furniture create an
unmistakable Scandinavian
look – one that has been
emulated all over the world.

village houses have front and back gardens, whereas
European village houses tend to rise up straight from
the side of the street or a very narrow pavement.
Another difference is that precisely because so many
Continental hill (or at least hilly) villages have
streets and houses tightly packed together, there has
been little opportunity to extend houses, so that
many more buildings are in their original state, bar
a few added modern services, not very subtly
installed because of the thick stone walls.

In America, the East Coast, Mid-West and some
southern states village houses, like British ones, often
have small front gardens enclosed, particularly on
the East Coast, by neat white picket fences, and are
generally positioned on wider, tree-lined streets.
Most of the houses are covered in clapboard painted
white, with certainly a porch somewhere or other,

so there is a pleasing harmony. In fact, such villages
moved James Fenimore Cooper to rapture when he
visited the region after a trip to Europe. 'New England
may justly glory in its villages! In space, freshness, an
air of neatness and comfort, they far exceed anything
I have ever seen, even in the mother country… I have
passed in one day, six or seven of these beautiful,
tranquil and enviable looking hamlets, for not one
of which I have been able to recollect an equal in the
course of my European travelling'.

the practicalities

Wherever the village, whatever the style and period,
most of the houses have everything in common
with cottages situated in more bucolic situations,
however fanciful. Rooms do not have generous
proportions, ceilings are low, windows are small,

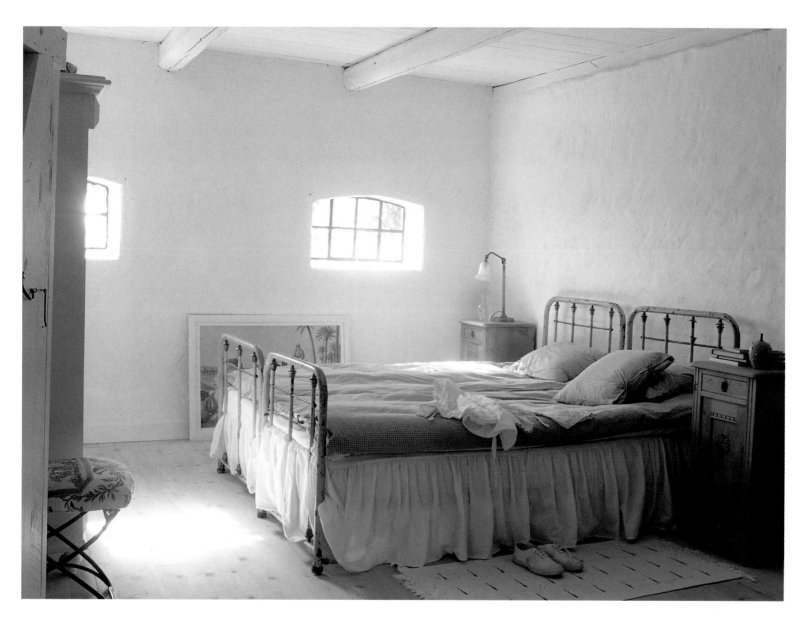

chimneys and fireplaces are often large. Renovations and conversions need to be focused on improving the feeling of space and light, if not the square footage, although it is often possible when gardens exist to extend rooms outwards. Just as many outbuildings can be properly joined to the main house and turned into a useful small room, such as a utility room, shower room, even a kitchen, thus freeing the original rooms for reception and sleeping purposes. If walls between rooms are not load-bearing, they can be removed to make larger spaces. Rooms will look and feel bigger if the floors, walls and furniture are pale, particularly if a reasonable amount of light comes through windows. It is often possible to turn attics hitherto used for storage into usable bedrooms by removing the ceiling to expose the rafters above (making sure

to install or improve insulation in the process), and adding dormer windows that should be quite in keeping. Check that the roof tiles are in good repair and replace any worn or broken ones.

Irremediably dark, small rooms should be made cosier with rich, warm paint, a relatively easy task with such a good choice now of historic paint colours and fabrics. It is cheering to think that many warm, dark rooms look best filled with furniture and pattern. The smaller the house, the more comfortable it needs to be, so make sure that heating, lighting and plumbing are as good as possible; the same applies to mattresses and upholstery. Make sure, too, that windows, doors and walls are draught-proof by filling in gaps and installing better-fitting windows and doors in keeping with the period. The same applies to filling in gaps between floorboards.

above

Simple rooms, simple architecture, simple but practical furnishings – such a mantra is essential when renovating a village cottage. To a certain extent, this also applies to larger village houses, although with these, especially the finely detailed 18th-century houses, you will have more latitude. Even though it is simply furnished, this bedroom is seductive in its almost purist way.

right

The new kitchen, together with the new dining room, is now the busy centre of the house. The walls were deliberately aged a straw colour to look as if they had been there for decades.

swedish style

When Martin and Edie van Breems first set eyes on their Connecticut farmhouse it was half-burned down and mainly roofless. The rough hewn beams in the remaining small, low-ceilinged rooms were blackened with smoke, there was major water damage and all the wiring and plumbing needed replacing. It was not, therefore, a particularly prepossessing project.

However, since Martin van Breems is an inventor and manufacturer of sailboat hardware and experienced at boat-building, and his wife a distinguished dealer in 18th- and 19th-century Swedish furniture, they were probably less deterred than most. They both saw the possibilities and opportunities in the farmhouse and were determined to preserve or restore its original character as appropriate. Their only real caveat was the small, dark rooms that remained, so they decided to redress the balance by adding on a generous kitchen and dining room with a master bedroom above in ▶

location: Fairfile, Connecticut, USA

built: c.1760, enlarged 1820, 20th-century addition

revived: Early 21st century

above

Another view of the new kitchen with its many windows and impressive collection of plants. Between the windows is a typical Swedish Mora longcase clock. Although most of the furniture is antique Swedish, the dining chairs are reproduction with leather seats.

right

A 1770s Gustavian settee with Louis Seize Neo-Classical lines is grouped with more Rococo-style Gustavian armchairs in the sitting room, originally a dining room, in the old part of the house. Checked and striped upholstery complements the 18th-century framework well.

left

Another view of the sitting room shown on page 129, with its simple fireplace, dove-grey walls, carved mirror and sconces. Although there is more daylight filling the new rooms, the atmosphere created in the old rooms is very similar.

left

A yellow-painted 18th-century Gustavian settee in the old parlour is a variation on English Chippendale furniture. The wide floorboards are left bare and uncluttered, as they are in most of the rooms.

left

A charming bedroom in the old part of the house with even more examples of the superb collection of Swedish 18th- and 19th-century furniture. The couronne bed treatment behind the bedhead adds just the right amount of softness to the mostly bare floorboards and heavily beamed walls and ceiling.

below

A marble-topped washstand in a bathroom that has been painted the same mellow wall colour as the bedroom shown on the left. The handsome greyed-gilt mirror and mushroom prints propped casually against the wall suit the room well. The pot of narcissi adds a requisite freshness.

the same general feeling of the original house, which had been built by one of the town's founding fathers. 'Interestingly,' they said, 'it was the 20th-century additions to the house that had collapsed. The original parts proved far more sturdy.'

To help blend the lighter and much airier new part with the old, they managed to salvage some chunky beams from a dairy barn in the Hudson River Valley and ordered 18th-century-style windows similar to the originals. They then gave the new walls the patina of age by slathering on a kind of cement or plaster (known in the trade as 'basic brown coat'), into which they had added pigment to tint the texture dove-grey or straw-yellow – colours 'that hold the shadows and always seem to be bathed in candlelight'. The end result is a home that successfully combines the light and spacious with the warm and intimate. Better still, it is the perfect foil for the enviable collection of Gustavian furniture that looks equally well in all the rooms, new and old.

conversions

6

Clearly, one needs imagination,

optimism and, not least in any

way, courage, before embarking

on the venture of turning a

building meant for some quite

other purpose into a home.

Old agricultural and industrial

buildings, schools, chapels

and churches are all prime

candidates for such a change of

role, especially because of the

generous space they offer and

their comparatively low prices.

the meaning of conversion

In the non-technical sense 'conversion' means a change in function, such as turning a school into a home or an animal shelter into an extra living room. In technical jargon it means a 'material change of use'. 'Conversion' is also often used instead of 'renovation'. For example, you might say, 'I am converting an old cottage', meaning you are restoring yet modernizing it to attain the comfortable standards of modern life. In this chapter 'conversion' means primarily a change in function or use, though it also takes in major improvements to unusual dwellings that may have had substandard living quarters.

There are many people for whom it is anathema to be tied by the building rules and regulations entangling period houses. Others desire more living space than it is normally possible to find in regular old houses or apartments. What such people usually have in common is the desire to find an idiosyncratic existing building whose interior they can transform and experiment with whatever their imagination and financial ability will allow. These are the people who need to find a building that has never before been domesticated, never before been a home. It could be that they are looking for a house that was merely an appendage to a working building, which means they can expand into the latter in an interesting way – a lighthouse, for example, or an old school building. Then again, they might consider a deconsecrated church or chapel or a convent, priory or monastery, even though these are, of course, former dwellings.

For the most part, whatever appropriate building these idiosyncrasy-seekers manage to find, it will mostly be involved in, as planning officers say, 'a change of use'. This means there will still be rules and regulations to follow as there are for any 'material changes of use', and in most countries some sort of planning permission will be required. But generally the rules and regulations will not be nearly as stringent as they would be for an existing dwelling, especially if it is of significant age, or is listed as

being of particular interest. More to the point, there will be much more latitude for the redesign of the interiors as long as they do not 'materially change' the outside, at least, of any treasured or historic building, or any old building 'in the public eye', however rarely seen. I know of a barn in southern England that is almost a mile up a private drive from the nearest road, and on private property, but because it is also on the edge of a designated public footpath, permission was refused for a major conversion. This included the installation of a very large window at the back in place of the old entrance, which was big enough to allow the passage of a horse and cartload of hay, to take advantage of the outstanding view.

above

The veranda shades an old railway carriage, converted into a single-storey dwelling.

right

This old stone and wood barn has a gentle rural situation, stunning internal roof structure, masses of space and an extremely pleasing exterior, which has been only very gently altered.

the building

The kind of buildings that lend themselves to a total change of use are immensely varied. By now we are all familiar with lofts – the huge neglected floors of industrial urban buildings that are no longer needed for industry. New York City has made them famous, first as splendid studio spaces for painters, sculptors and photographers, and then as desirable real estate for the savvy.

Today, old city industrial buildings are keenly sought after around the world; barns are as well. Old agricultural buildings no longer needed for hay storage, animals or agricultural machinery are favourites for their often enviable rural locations and their stunning internal roof structure, if the barn is of any age. Bear in mind that it is often more difficult to obtain permission to convert barns, especially ancient ones, than other types of building. However, there is a thriving trade in barn transfers, not just from one part of a country to another, but from one country to another, all the dismantled pieces and beams being meticulously marked and numbered for identical reassembly.

Then there are empty churches, convents, monasteries and chapels; school halls and school buildings themselves; meeting houses; old shops and garages; stables, haylofts and granaries; boathouses and lumbering barges; Chinese junks; firehouses and lighthouses; animal shelters; abandoned railway stations; byres with haylofts above, even dovecotes and *pigeonniers* (pigeon lofts), which are greatly prized in France; Martello towers (the watchtowers set up at intervals on much of the English coast as lookout posts and first defences during the Napoleonic campaigns when the fear of invasion was rife); light-industry factories, blacksmith's workshops and forges; and the various types of old mill, from watermills to flour mills, almost invariably found in picturesque spots beside a river or stream – the list of buildings that can be converted into a home is extensive.

the approach

It has to be said that there are almost as many different ways of approaching the renovation of these various conversions (including water-based structures) as there are such buildings themselves. The same is true of renovating regular houses, as much depends upon locality, climate and the age of the structure as well as on your budget and the particular needs of your family.

As far as old structures are concerned, the approach that you take when converting a property can be much the same as the three approaches discussed on pages 80–5, but with one addition. As well as renovating a building in a 'reverential' way, an 'innovative' way, or, if it is feasible and your budget is small (although, because of the nature of the exercise, this is rarely an option), in a 'cosmetic' way, there is a fourth way, especially for major renovations. This is the 'honest', or Modernist, way.

above

This dining area formed part of a French monastic chapel. The dominating wooden triangle is not an original feature but part of an old dependent farm building.

left

This bedroom is in an apartment converted from a London hospital built in the 1840s. The converters were careful to retain or restore all the Victorian Gothic details, or, if they were too far gone or missing, to commission faithful reproductions.

There is not much point in being truly reverential with most major renovations, and in any case the extent of the project more or less prevents it. When the structure is an old barn, barge, junk, Martello tower, *pigeonnier*, lighthouse, boathouse, mill or old religious building, a reverential lover of old buildings will try to be sensitive to the existing wood, stone or brick, the roof pitch, the roof details, the guttering, the doors and particularly, as always, to those great giveaways, the windows. In general, this group will try to keep original windows and/or find similar windows (or have them custom-made), and to add more fenestration if it is needed and allowed. They will retain the original door openings, and will make every effort to replace missing bricks or stones with carefully selected old ones as near as possible in period as well as look to the originals. Rotten timbers will be relieved of their duties by rescued old beams or planks in better condition. In the case of an ancient barn that would not have had any original glazing, the renovators will insert plain, fixed glass as far as possible, maybe with wooden louvres, to look as much like the old glassless, shuttered or louvred windows as they can make them. In short, every effort will be made to retain every element of the original character. When all is finished the owners can sit happily inside and take delight in their glorious roof structure.

Other reverential converters will try to domesticate whatever old structure they have found, to turn it into a mellow-looking dwelling as nearly as possible true to its spirit and period. To do this with any chance of success requires a great deal of knowledge, a lot of research, luck in finding original materials, and the imagination, stamina and skill to complete the task. Many people would be horrified by the 'dishonesty' of such an exercise, raising the argument for 'modern buildings for modern times'. Yet these objectors may live in a 1940s dead ringer for an early 18th-century colonial

house, or a 'modern' house based on a Bauhaus design coming up to 100 years old. To counter this view, it could be pointed out that when a large part of Windsor Castle was burnt down it was restored as nearly as possible to its original self on the premise that the many tourists to Windsor would expect the ancient, even as partly a replica.

Innovators are most likely to search for buildings with which they can more or less do what they like: old stores, warehouses, lofts, railway stations, Victorian mills and industrial buildings where they can have free rein in the space at their disposal. If they are historically minded and with a taste for

above

Most of the old architectural details have been left in this restored and converted theatre. The addition of the steel staircase, glass-sided balcony, squared-off windows and unadorned polished floor, as well as the sculpture, has turned an old building into a very modern space.

the fanciful they might try to turn a 19th-century building into one of the 19th-century rural pastiches much favoured at the time and extolled (with patterns) in contemporary books such as John Plaw's *Fermes Ornés and Rural Improvements* (1800) and John Loudon's indispensable *Encyclopaedia of Cottage, Farm and Villa Architecture* (1833). This might seem rather like building a film set, but the early 19th century was the period of pastiches, as well as of Neo-Classicism, which at a stretch could be said to have been something of a pastiche as well. So in this sense such a folly would be correctly reminiscent of the spirit of the times.

Sometimes the exterior will be left in much the same manner as it was built (tidied up and restored, of course), to give visitors a surprise as they step through the front door into whatever fantasy or soaring modern space the architect and owner have conceived for the inside. In other cases, the original structure will be subsumed in some total innovation, left to act only as the framework for the new whole.

above

To the uninformed eye there is nothing to indicate that the interior of this restored chapel in Turin has been domesticated, which must lead to some unexpected intrusions from time to time.

right

The interior of the chapel shown above reveals how a place of worship has been transformed into a home, with various living areas built on several different levels. The original carved chapel doors make a suitably grand entrance.

the time & expense

The cosmetic approach is almost impossible to pull off in a conversion because of the structural work and installation of modern services needed. Probably the most one could hope for is to do the minimum of repair and reconstruction to the exterior and to concentrate resources on the interior. Any exterior faults and ugliness can in many cases be partially disguised by quick-growing climbers.

The fourth approach – the 'honest', Modernist 'let's create something that is for and of our own time out of this old detritus of a building' – was prevalent during the 20th century and in the worst cases led to the destruction of much that was pleasant and well crafted. In the best cases, however, it produced some stunningly innovative work.

What must always be borne in mind is that many of the buildings that lend themselves to conversion will require almost as much work and money spent on them (and maybe more of both) as building a new house from scratch – probably just about all the work that will be saved is the process of digging holes for setting the foundations. A correspondingly extensive amount of imagination will also be needed to achieve that final splendid space of your dreams, usually unobtainable in more conventional dwellings.

Many buildings will need to have windows inserted, as well as fireplaces and chimneys. Gutters might need to be replaced and maybe roofs, too, or at the very minimum roof tiles; crumbling walls may need strengthening or rebuilding – the least you might need to do is provide a great deal of insulation. Oversize door openings may have to be kept to conform with regulations. Internal doors will nearly always have to be provided, for even the most open of open-plan living will need doors for bathrooms and lavatories. Staircases will be required if there are two or more floors. And the floors themselves may have to be replaced or updated. Most buildings will require new plumbing, and probably water will have to be laid on as well, quite apart from heating and wiring. It is crucial to find out before starting work – in fact, even before buying – how easy it will be to install water, electricity, a telephone line and so on, if the building is far from main services.

All of these things will have to be done with the same imagination and sensitivity as required for old period houses – probably rather more, since there is little in the way of guidance for domesticating, say, a former light-engineering factory. Prospective owners need vision and the confidence to pull off their dream project.

right

A converted storeroom has now become a valuable part of this 18th-century farmhouse. The stone floor is a charming original feature, as are the windows and wooden beams.

left

This splendid grid screen wall of a former warehouse is now part of a thoroughly modern kitchen, with the twin stainless-steel sinks and apron suspended over shelves. The vertical mullions, which form part of the original grid wall, are wide enough for hanging the occasional picture.

left
This slickly executed corridor is the former lower level of the monastery's cloister and is in stark contrast to the upper level shown on page 145. The heavily beamed ceiling and the old ecclesiastical bench are, however, worthy reminders of a historical and religious past.

location: Le Muy, Var, France

built: 10th–18th century

revived: Late 1990s

above

The gently slumbering front of the old monastery, now called Château Sainte Roseline and a prestigious vineyard. The row of urns in front of the bank of long, graceful windows, are the rare 18th-century vases d'Anduze. The garden is a lovely combination of lushness and formality.

asceticism reinterpreted

left

The dining room, which leads off the new kitchen, is furnished with designs by the architect Jean-Michel Wilmotte, except, that is, for the art and the old olive jar.

Looking at the beautiful, tranquil façade of this venerable former monastery, admiring the rhythm of the two floors of graceful shuttered windows punctuated by the row of box-filled vases d'Anduze, it is really hard to imagine that the interior has been almost entirely reconstructed. In fact, the mainly 18th-century religious property, which actually dates right back to the 1300s, was bought as a vineyard a few years ago by Françoise and Bernard Teillaud in order to produce the prestigious Château Sainte Roseline wines. The Teillauds then promptly commissioned the architect Jean-Michel Wilmotte to totally revamp the more or less ruined interior, a task that he accomplished with considerable élan as well as sensitivity, designing most of the furniture as well as rearranging the interior spaces.

Crisp, pure lines, a disciplined simplicity, excellent new lighting and an eclectic choice of art, which, although sophisticated and edgy when taken as individual components, result, en masse, in an empathetic reinterpretation of the old monastic asceticism. ▶

right

Jean-Michel Wilmotte's
interesting solution for the
new kitchen is like half a room
within a room, or perhaps a
kind of stage set for the useful
banks of storage drawers and
the *batterie de cuisine*.

left

Black-edged and framed doors
lead the eye through an
impressive enfilade of rooms
from the new dining room.
This detail of black edging
works very well with the crisp
pure lines of the furniture.

right
The cool and spacious master bedroom is flooded with natural light streaming in through the long, graceful windows that look so covetable from the outside. The skeletal four-poster and chair suit the style and mood of the room perfectly.

below
The religious origins of the building are very much in evidence in the upper level of the ancient cloister.

This is an asceticism that is in deliberate contrast to the mellowness and ancient charm of the sleepy exterior and garden with its ancient and huge trees, but nevertheless an integral part of the whole – as it must always have been.

One of the most interesting juxtapositions is the deliberate contrast between the top and bottom parts of the old cloister: the top section has been left much as it must always have been, while the bottom is as sleek a piece of modern architectural purity as there can be. Then there are the lovingly engineered vistas – slivers of views of the lush outside through windows and graceful interior vistas through the carefully balanced enfilades of rooms. Whichever way you look at the new lease of life given to this former monastery, the end result is indeed a stunning achievement.

left

For a couple of painters who needed inspiring studio space as well as a living area, an old cinema, latterly an amusement arcade, on a seashore promontory in Scotland was a gift from the gods. The original pitch-black interior has been replaced by a spacious studio with huge windows, a minimalist mezzanine living area and a stunning sea view.

right

This rural-looking but somewhat skeletal structure was originally an industrial building in a park-like area in Paris. Replacing some of the walls with glass but retaining, obviously, the structural members has produced an extraordinarily rustic feeling.

the interiors

Interestingly, there tend not to be as many outstanding differences in the interiors of the various kinds of conversion as you might imagine there to be. If the exteriors are kept, for the most part, to their original styles or periods, with such alterations as are allowed for modern-day domestic purposes, the interiors (depending, of course, on the space and budget available and the taste of the owners and that of the architect/designer) will frequently be open-plan. It is quite common for kitchens to become

part of the living area, with only bedrooms and bathrooms given any privacy. Some sort of original, either deliberately industrial, or designed to be, elegant staircase could rise up from the living area as a focal point. If the space is high, as it generally is, the staircase could ascend in a series of landings and galleries from which one would be able to look down to the living area or up to the exposed joists of some splendid roof trusses. An open-tread staircase in reinforced glass, wood or steel, with stretched steel cords, steel halyards or Perspex could take the place of the traditional balustrade.

White-painted walls are a popular option, and they could perhaps be lined with old tongue-and-groove or matchstick boarding. As for floors, reclaimed boards or battered boards painted white suit conversions particularly well. Alternatively, the floor could be brick or Mexican or Italian terracotta tiles, polished concrete, limestone, coir or sisal, or even marble. If there is a real noise or heat problem, the floor could be covered with a good old-fashioned carpet, perhaps with a scattering of kelims. Woodwork could be painted in with the walls or stained a bright colour, sometimes matched by any exposed pipework.

The type of furniture that usually works best in converted properties is either modern classic with the occasional quirky touch, or very eclectic. Generally, the whole point of buying such a building for conversion is to gain as much space as possible, so you could have some massive armoires, mammoth tables and so on, which you can probably buy for a song because few other people will have enough room for them.

Sophisticated, unfussy lighting tends to suit converted properties, with the latest in recessed spots if there is any sort of ceiling recess; if there is none, opt for very carefully placed wall- or ceiling-mounted versions. Uplighters and dimmer switches, backed up by interesting, sometimes industrial lamps, can create flexible ambient lighting. Ideal upholstery is often simple and modern, either white, cream or stone-coloured 'duck' or canvas, or some sort of tan *faux* suede or leather, or occasionally in assorted fondant colours.

A judicious selection of interesting paintings and prints could be artfully displayed, and maybe a collection of exceptional 20th-century black-and-white photographs. Accessories and objects need to be carefully chosen but they can be as fascinating as the paintings. And you could easily include pieces of sculpture, whether old or new.

Almost inevitably, conversions include French doors or sliding or folding glass doors opening out on to a terrace, veranda or deck, or even just grass or a beach, depending on the structure and its location. If permitted by local regulations, as large an area of glass as possible could be added to an old barn or a mill to take full advantage of their charming locations. A well-lit mill race streaming and frothing its way down the bed of a river or stream and filling a window with the sight is almost like having it in the room itself. Old industrial buildings, too, can enjoy romantic views of the city, particularly at night, which again might be maximized with stupendous windows.

These are very 21st-century spaces furnished in a very 21st-century style that is amazingly universal. They are quite pure in a way, spare without being minimalist, pleasant to live in, easy to maintain and easy on the eye. But, of course there are exceptions to these generalizations: smaller, skinnier, idiosyncratic spaces chosen more for their stunning positions than their generous potential square footage, like, for example, a lighthouse, boathouse, Martello tower, water tower, windmill, an old barge, even a boat, for that matter. These spaces will, of course, need a kitchen, at least one bedroom and bathroom, a living area and perhaps a laundry room fitted, and all too often in the most peculiar of spaces. The rooms created may, inconveniently, need to be on different levels, in order to have them at all. In the case of converted boats, it behoves designers to test every trick in the trade to increase the headroom, by

above
Like most converted barns, this one has a mezzanine upper floor, with all the benefit of extra light and a view from an enormous window carved right out of the eaves. The downstairs, too, is hardly short of natural light, with its many side windows, sometimes on two levels. The space is large enough for a massive sofa and dining table beyond.

right
The metal walkway of a former industrial building has been retained, giving character to a spacious, clean-cut and wonderfully light and airy living space. With a panoramic city view, it is no wonder that properties like this are in such great demand.

raising ceilings, even in the middle of a room, if that is feasible, and creating wells, wherever possible, in floors. Even the smallest break in a surface, above or below, creates at least an illusion of more space.

These smaller and, generally speaking, older spaces lend themselves to lighting that is deliberately less than chic. Retro light fittings and lamps, or even just oil lamps and candles complement them perfectly, especially in areas where it has proved difficult and often horrifyingly expensive to garner an electricity supply or even that standby, a generator set.

Enormous spaces, like deconsecrated churches or warehouses or former school buildings will need to have divisions and mezzanine floors and partition walls added, rather than subtracted, in order to make domestic sense of the area. Acoustics, too, will need to be dealt with by installing as many soft surfaces as possible to absorb the echoing sounds that beset such cavernous buildings. New owners of old stables, cowsheds and so on may decide to make use of some of the existing partitions, but also introduce floors using different materials and windows not strictly authentic but in the style of the building. A prolonged and vigorous airing, a fresh resurfacing of walls and some appropriate ventilation may be required to get rid of any residual animal smells.

The somewhat spare interiors I have described above are by no means always *de rigueur*. I came across a marvellous shop and back-room conversion recently, complete with rooms above, that was a riot of colour with mixtures of fabric and *faux* jewels pinned to the walls, and every one of the old treads of the stairs a different colour, not to mention the banisters. And I will always remember a converted warehouse where the walls of the main living area were an extraordinary collage of layers of different-coloured tissue paper pasted one above the other with random exuberance – the effect was truly magical. The furniture was mostly painted, and eccentric enough to befit this wonderland world.

left

Old boats, barges and junks
make more than credible,
and sometimes very
spacious, homes for those
who love to be on the water.
This bathroom in a
converted boat is beautifully
fitted out with a generous
amount of copper trim,
elegantly curved at one end,
around the bath tub.

In both cases the original buildings had been
resurrected and infused with a dramatically
different new life and identity.

In the course, though, of looking at many different
conversions, I have been struck by those exceptions
when clearly furniture and furnishings have been
chosen to suit a given space rather than the original
structure, and in some cases, position. One might,
for example, suppose that those who convert
churches and other ecclesiastical buildings might
veer towards the Gothic for their chosen style. Or
that domesticators of barns and other agricultural
buildings would choose a rustic or at least rural look.
But this happens less often than you might think.
Owners of churches and chapels are just as likely to
go for industrial chic as loft buyers, or a bookish,
literary feel rather than an ascetic one. Converted
barns are frequently a whole lot more sophisticated
than bucolic, while former industrial buildings can

look positively luxurious if not exactly cosy. However,
I have stayed in a so-called 'beach house' restoration,
admittedly a rather grand one, where the walls were
lined with velvet and the floors so highly polished
that the merest grain of escaped sand would have
caused havoc. There was absolutely no attempt at all
to incorporate any casual 'I do like to be beside the
seaside' factor. So the old adage about 'suitability,
suitability, suitability' being the criteria for an
appropriate choice of styles does not always hold
true, especially for those with the confidence and
originality to do what they like, regardless.

Nevertheless, these examples are, in the main, all
exceptions to the rule. Sensitivity to the period of a
building without being totally slavish to that period,
or at least sensitivity to a building's potential
depending upon your needs, the 'feeling' of the
building and its situation, are still important points
to bear in mind when converting a building.

above

An imaginative use of space
has been made in this boat
conversion, with children's
bunk beds tucked away
behind a dividing arch.

above left

Situated right on the water,
boathouses make good
domestic conversions. In this
light-filled boathouse, with its
tongue-and-groove ceiling,
narrow partitions separate
the different areas. Extra
light is thrown up from the
white-painted wooden floor.

atlantic lighthouse

Three generations of the Wyeth family have been great painters of the craggy, windswept, salt-soaked Maine coast. It seems only fitting that Jamie Wyeth, son of Andrew and Betsy Wyeth, and grandson of N. C. Wyeth, should live and work in a mid-19th-century lighthouse. Situated on a private island off the Maine coast, the secluded lighthouse is a 30-minute row to the mainland.

Jamie's grandfather brought his family to Port Clyde on the mainland in 1920, and in 1978 Andrew and Betsy Wyeth bought and began the restoration of the lighthouse, abandoned some 45 years before. In 1994, Jamie bought the lighthouse and the surrounding 23 acres from his parents, and continued the renovation process with his

below

Rounded walls with shuttered windows in the simply furnished dining area look as appealing from the inside as they do from the outside. The table is surrounded by sturdy captain's chairs and surmounted by four antique lightning rods.

wife Phyllis, who spends a good deal of time in the couple's other home in Pennsylvania. In the process, they turned what Andrew Wyeth called his 'Elba' into a haven rather than a place of exile, and Jamie became a real lighthouse buff in the process.

The outside and the foundations were solid enough and although the interior in some ways deliberately reflects the austere surroundings, it is reassuringly comfortable, with leather-covered sofas (used as beds by former lighthouse keepers on night watch), handwoven blankets, leather-bound books, hook rugs, masses of squashy pillows and a collection of 'lighthouse items' enthusiastically put together by Jamie. All this and a fireplace, too, making it as good for Jamie to be there in winter as in other seasons.

above

The metronome-shaped building facing out to sea is the bell tower – now entirely spick-and-span, not to mention shipshape – which preceded the foghorn used today.

right

The collective lighthouse buildings, set just back from the rocky shore, are weather-boarded and painted a sparkling white. Partly ringed by trees, the property is actually a mile from the dock and another half an hour's row to the mainland.

location: Southern Island, Maine, USA

built: *c.* 1860

revived: 1978 and mid-1990s

right

The living area has a
comfortable well-worn feel,
with its plumped-up cushions,
hooked rugs and seafaring
and lighthouse memorabilia.
The whole scene appears to be
framed in white.

above

'A lighthouse,' says Jamie Wyeth,
'is the quintessence of Maine.'
To all intents and purposes, this
photograph confirms his words
as fact. All the wildness, valour,
sea mists and saltiness, sun-
bleached timbers and great
changing skies are contained
within this evocative vignette.

right

The bedrooms may be spare in
feeling but they do not lack any
physical comforts. A great pile
of pillows on the bed, creature
comforts to the side – what
more could a person need?

holiday homes

7

In many ways, holiday or vacation homes are the most pleasurable homes to look for and renovate. There is no real sense of urgency – after all, you do not have to own one, and it does not have to be the house of your dreams. Nor does it have to be near work or schools. It is a place for relaxation in a location that you particularly enjoy.

getting away

As long as you can find a property at the right price in an ideal area that faces in your preferred direction, with a good feel about it and a pleasant aspect, with the right amount of space for you to hang out and entertain in, you have, theoretically, got it made…

The trouble with such leisure homes (for that is what they are meant for and should be) is that if you already have a house that you are proud of, it is unlikely that you will settle for second best when choosing another. Or if you do make compromises – because, for example, the place has a breathtaking view and is positioned in exactly the spot you had always dreamed of – it will be with the proviso that you will be able to improve or, at the very least, cosmeticize it outside and make it exactly how you want inside. Even if this is not possible, you can at least make your holiday home as comfortable and as easy to run as possible. After all, your guests are unlikely to expect anything more than comfortable casual, so details such as no cellphone connection, an erratic television reception and chancy plumbing will not drive them away if there are other incentives.

Just *being* in your holiday home, with all the different amenities from those of everyday life, should be ample compensation for any lack of modern conveniences. In any case, there is something peculiarly comforting about sun-faded fabrics and somewhat shabby furniture that can be messed up and ill-treated by children and adults who should know better, when you do not have to live with it all year round. If that is too much to contemplate for the truly houseproud, simple, sturdy furnishings, with deeply comfortable

mattresses, a good reading light and an excellent shower are quite irresistible. These last three attributes are the things to strive for, whatever else goes by the board. Oh, and you would probably prefer to have a decent fireplace or woodburning stove (for nowhere has perfect weather all the time), good cooking facilities, a dishwasher, washing machine and dryer.

left

This American beach house deck could hardly be more geared to minimal maintenance. It is simplicity itself with a shingle roof, tongue-and-groove cedar floor and easy indoor-outdoor Lloyd Loom chairs. These are also absolutely in keeping with the age and style of the house.

right

Old beach houses, perched, quite literally if you look at the supporting piers, on the edge of the stony shore in Novia Scotia. Protection from the stormy seas and high winds is essential in such vulnerable positions, so the houses are well weather-proofed. Note the traditional gables and chimneys, small windows and clapboard exteriors – the design has changed very little from the 17th century.

left

This is a true inside-outside holiday home in Mexico. Large, square terracotta tiles are laid in an uninterrupted flow from the house through to the generously planted terrace, where the furnishings are much the same colours as those inside. The hammock, slung from the columns, gives a pleasantly airy alternative to the bed.

right

This holiday home terrace in a village in southern Europe is an integral part of the setting, with its surrounding rooftops, church tower and views of the mountains. Indeed, it was the renovator's firm intention to keep the house as much in context with its neighbouring buildings as possible.

the right position

Once you have established that it can be made adequately comfortable, the most important plus for a holiday home should be its irrefutably wonderful position. Think: 'position, position, position' because that truly is the most important catchphrase to guide you towards the best holiday home, just as 'suitability, suitability, suitability' is the essential catchphrase for any successful renovation of an old house, particularly for the exterior.

From a practical point of view, it is a good idea to look around at neighbouring houses. If most of them look rather alike and your new purchase stands out as being totally dissimilar, however beautiful the setting, then I think that you should try to make it fit in with the general feel of the locality and ambience. Just as a pastel-coloured façade (no matter how charming the colour) in a terrace of white stucco or old redbrick houses would be a glaring mistake, so, too, would a beach house dolled up with bright white paint, window-boxes and hanging baskets of plants on the American East Coast, when all the surrounding houses are unadorned weather-greyed shingle or clapboard. However nice the house, it could not help but look pretentious and incongruous. On the other hand, that same white-painted house with its dazzle of flowering plants would look perfectly appropriate on the coasts of California, Florida, Australia or the Mediterranean, where the simple shingled or clapboard houses would look sadly drab.

Whatever else you have to be sensitive about, you will not have to be reverential. Such a quality in a holiday house is a contradiction in terms. Unless your holiday home happens to be in the heart of an old European village, in which case it is just being there that counts, what you do want to insist upon is a glorious view of wherever you happen to be – whether by sea, lake or river, in charming country, or near snowy (or flower-covered) mountains. The interior of the home has to be in context, too, so that the character of your holiday location is always apparent.

humble beginnings

Not many people can boast, if it is a boast, that they live in a converted pigsty, even if that pigsty was formerly a sheep pen, which, in turn, was originally a mid-19th-century farm. But if position is everything, this basic, two-roomed cottage has it all.

Originally the building had a thatched roof and sash windows, but both were replaced in the 1930s when the side gables were lowered, the tin roof added and the columns on the porch constructed. It was bought and restored very recently as a holiday home for Paul Duncan, the editor of South African *House & Garden*. There is no electricity, but there is gas for cooking and paraffin lamps for night; water is piped to the house across the veld from a waterfall more than two miles away. The main attractions are the undoubted beauty and the changing colours of the landscape, the peace, the silence, the pure, pure air and the extraordinary sense of space. ▶

location: The Karoo, South Africa

built: *c.*1850

revived: 1930s, 2001

right

The shuttered windows look out across the veld to a mountain in the distance. The house, with its over-scale chimney, is a brilliant white in contrast to the surrounding landscape.

left

Although the cottage is small and looks even smaller against the huge stretch of veld, there is a certain unexpected grandeur in the columns and arch of the porch. From the inside, looking out, they frame the mountains with a becoming sense of drama.

above

The kitchen-living room is simply but adequately furnished and equipped. Anything more elaborate would have been quite out of character with the simple structure and the kind of life that is lived in the house.

The house has extremely thin interior walls, and these have been dazzlingly whitewashed, as have the exterior walls. The ceilings are the originals, made from reeds that were collected from local rivers. One of the most labour-intensive jobs was getting them free of the years and years of black soot that clung to them; this required careful and seemingly endless washing with sugar-water. The other major renovation job was to resurface the dung floors. The front door originally belonged to another derelict farm nearby, and the intention is to replace the current metal-framed windows with windows that are more to the scale of the shutters. Other than that, the furnishings are as simple and basic as the structure itself – and all that was needed.

right

Like the rest of the house, the bedroom is simply but comfortably furnished. Note the original reeded ceiling.

in the mountains

There is not an enormous amount of variation in ski lodges and chalets except in size and comfort level. Basically what you want is a good, comfortable living/eating space with a vast fireplace (with storage space for firewood) and neat bedrooms with bathrooms off them. The kitchen can be planned with a countertop opening onto the living area for optimum sociability, and big freezer space for food supplies if the nearest shops are far away.

The view from a ski lodge or chalet is nearly always spectacular, so you will want the largest possible windows all around that are compatible with the minimum possible heat loss. Wooden walls inside and out mean that decoration can be

right

One of the points about using wood to build in mountain climates is that the material expands and contracts with extremes of heat and cold, hence the need for well-seasoned planks that will stand up to the weather. The split planks and beams here seem ripe for repair and were, perhaps, installed before the requisite ageing process.

left

This typical mountain chalet has windows all around to take maximum advantage of the views. The bottom part of the building is well lagged against the winter snow and possible floods from the stream.

far right

This American log cabin more or less maintains itself. The furnishings are kept deliberately simple, with the old snowshoes and straw hat displayed on the wall reflecting the seasons of the locality. The arched door is an unexpected, but rather charming, touch.

kept to a minimum, and floors should be well sealed to offer maximum protection against snow brought in on boots and coats. You will want generous storage space for bulky skiwear, outer clothes and boots as well as skis – ideally, this should be a room with an exterior door to minimize the need to drag wet boots through the house. Remember to pay close attention to insulation as well as to the heating system.

Since water is rarely a problem in mountain areas, invest in the best showers available and roomy bathtubs for those who prefer a long soak, and make sure that you can rely on a constant supply of hot water – creature comforts are an absolute necessity after a hard day's skiing. Even if you use the house only during the spring and summer months, as opposed to winter, you will still want the same sense of comfort after long days spent hiking in the mountains.

on the water

'Oh, I do like to be beside the seaside,' goes the early twentieth-century song, which became a perennial favourite of holidaymakers. When the majority of people think of vacation houses they think of water and therefore of beach houses, and a significant number of them think of old beach houses. The nostalgic or wistful dream of so many people with memories of childhood vacations and sandy beaches stretching out blissfully into stunning sunsets, they do vary, once they are bought and renovated, as much as the moods of the sea itself.

Oceans and seas all over the world are lined with them: colonial houses with verandas on the Indian Ocean; chic 1920s and 1930s houses on the Mediterranean; long, cool, white houses with wraparound porches on both sides of the Pacific and the Tasman; more weatherbeaten, sun-bleached houses on the volatile Atlantic…

Just as holiday houses in general are comparatively easy to make decisions about because they tend to have a focused purpose, beach houses are simpler still, especially if they do not have to withstand harsh winters. In very hot climates the idea is to keep the house as cool as possible, and in cooler climates to attract as much sun as possible. All of them, whatever the sun allowance, need protection against the wear and tear of salty winds, mildew and rot. It is helpful to weatherproof them, at least against collected rain when the house is vacant, by having all the windowsills slightly sloping away from the window.

Many beach houses are built of wood, especially those in the Americas, the Tropics and the Antipodes, and almost all have some sort of porch, veranda, deck or terrace, and often balconies and sleep porches, too. Whatever their geographical origin, outdoor lounging, eating and space for the barbecue are almost as *de rigueur* as the beach itself. On the down side – and this is something that many beach houses share, whatever their size and

grandeur but especially if they are built on an island or on a remote coast – there may be problems with faulty plumbing and water shortages.

The great thing about old wooden houses is that they can be expanded very easily, and comparatively cheaply, provided that there is available surrounding land. Another room and bathroom here, a new sun porch there, a kitchen twice the size… It all takes place quite happily, and winter months are a hive of activity for carpenters, with the sound of saws and hammers replacing the summer cries of beach games.

The usual recommendations about renovation can generally go by the board when it comes to a beach house. The requirement to get to know and understand your building and to be sensitive to its

above

The old roof structure, wood columns and a highly decorative stripe of stained-glass squares at the tops of the windows were sensibly retained in this conversion of a former fisherman's cottage, with its all-around views of Sydney harbour.

right

A balcony bedroom has been neatly integrated into this airy old beach house in Greece. High ceilings mean that it is comparatively easy to make such alterations or room additions. Note that, as in France, the casement window opens inwards.

features is swept away by considerations about how to adapt the house or make room for yet another young married couple or grandchild. Old beach houses, especially those that have been in the same family for generations, are family homes in the true sense, and should be treated as such, so there is no need to be fussy about furnishings or floors.

Deal with the sharp scratches made by endless grains of sand by having floors that can be swept and mopped with ease and that will withstand drips from wet bathing suits and abandoned soggy towels. These include sealed and polyurethaned wooden floors, either painted or natural; non-slip tiles and, in smarter homes, limestone. Install an outdoor shower in a reasonably private place, for sluicing off as much sand as possible before going inside. Have a really efficient washing machine, dryer, refrigerator, freezer and dishwasher – all of which, as mentioned earlier, are essential for all family holiday houses. Install flyscreens at windows: either the ones that come complete as storm windows for winter and screens for summer, or the variety resembling blinds or shades that pull down from above the window and clip into metal grooves fixed down the sides of the frames and at the bottom.

As for the outside, regular maintenance is the wisest course. It is important to keep an eye on rotting wood and roofs and the state of window frames; keep the structure of the house as low maintenance yet as sturdy as possible to withstand the extremes of heat and cold. It is hard to think of storms and hurricanes in the hot blue of a summer's day, but they are apt to blow up in winter months when only a scattering of year-round residents are about and all the contractors have long lists of work ordered in the summer. So it is practical to install outside shutters that can be tightly fastened before you leave. If you can fix them over the doors as well, so much the better.

left

Slanting outdoor shutters are hugely important in this Thai holiday home. They filter the light, protect the interiors from the fierce sun and, at the same time, let in the maximum amount of air. They can also be bolted flat to secure the place when it is not in use. The high-panelled walls and ceilings also help to keep the house cool and airy.

right

The courtyard of this home in Cyprus provides a cool, shady place in which to relax while still enjoying the sights and sounds of the garden. The plastered walls and seating area have been painted a bold shade of lavender, which works beautifully in such a bright and verdant setting.

Those with a house by a lake or a river are likely to have some sort of boat as well, in which they spend a great deal of time. So there has to be somewhere to keep the boat and to lay it up when it is not going to be used. You may be lucky enough to find a place with a boathouse, but if not, you will need to acquire or build one.

Apart from the boat issue, many of the same conditions apply as for a beach house. Water is both a delight and a possible hazard, with the potential for flooding, if you are sited right by the water, that should not be discounted, especially for river houses. Not much can be done structurally to guard against this, except perhaps to look for a house on stilts or piers with a boathouse underneath. But you can at least renovate with this

possibility in mind. A good heating system is probably a necessity to keep damp at bay in the colder months, and, as in beach houses, serious attention should be given to roofs, gutters and exposed woodwork. Try to provide an airing cupboard with some sort of gentle heat to keep linens and towels from getting damp.

Floors need to be tough and easy to maintain, covered in tiles of some sort rather than wood, which could swell unless well sealed. Flooding apart, it is sensible to have floors that will withstand the damp and puddles from wet sailing clothes. Upholstery should be simple to clean, and the less fabric around, the better. Use shutters, blinds or shades instead of curtains. Furniture should be as reliably sturdy as possible.

left

The old boathouse doors open
out right onto the beach,
meaning that there is no need for
any sort of deck or terrace from
which to enjoy the sea views and
to soak up the general ambience.

right

One end of the light-filled living
area upstairs, with its handsome
ribbed ceiling and views all
around from the many windows.
The casual old furnishings have
been in place for many years and
have served respective owners
extremely well.

location: Felixstowe, England

built: 19th century

revived: mid-1980s

from boathouse to beach house

Boathouses are nearly always interesting structures, often spectacularly
sited, whether on the coast, a lake or a river, and more often than not there is enough
room inside to create somewhere to live. If not, there is often at least a suitable
structure at the side of the property to incorporate into the original. This boathouse
on the east coast of England was built in the 19th century and then turned into a
beach house sometime during the first half of the 20th century.

   An interesting fact about this building is that it was taken down at the beginning
of World War II and replaced by a gun emplacement, and then, after the war, it was
rebuilt to exactly the same specifications. The current owners bought the boathouse in
the mid-1980s, built another storey on top and merged the old boat shed alongside ▶

above

This view of the upstairs living area shows the staircase and the smaller windows at the end of the beach house. The prevailing colour is white, which suits the structure well, and understated so as not to compete with the sea and sky all around.

into the hallway to create extra living space. Apart from these modifications, the owners have retained all of the old elements, except for the stove, and even that is 'new old', so to speak, since it is a reclaimed 19th-century model. The floor, however, did need to be replaced, and the owners were fortunate to find similar tiles for sale in an old house in London, which they took up and transported to the coast where they then recreated the original pattern. You could call this a true labour of love – but a labour, after all, that is well within the tradition set by the original owners of simply replacing like with like.

left
The casually put-together kitchen, with its old wooden draining board and blue-and-white-tiled splashback. This, like the other rooms, is more serviceable than aesthetic and well within the deliberately casual beach-house tradition.

below
A detail of old stained-glass windows from the original 19th-century boathouse, now part of the hallway. The space has a definite Arts & Crafts feel about it.

As for the furnishings, these, too, were bought with the beach house more than 20 years ago, while all of the knick-knacks were foraged from local junk shops. In this, the owners were following a precedent set by so many old beach house owners or inheritors in many parts of the world: beach houses, unlike most other homes, are frequently sold complete with contents and topped up with this and that from car boot sales, jumble sales, local markets and junk shops. There is a kind of pride in preserving as battered and as casual and comfortable an 'old shoe' look as possible in such places, which are, after all, strictly for holidays and relaxing times.

glossary

When discussing a building, whatever its age, with an architect, builder, contractor or designer, it is useful to be familiar with the various architectural terms and styles. At the very least it is helpful to be able to look them up afterwards. It is especially useful to have some knowledge of building terms when studying quotes and bids for work to be undertaken. Certain influential architects and designers mentioned earlier in the book are also given some definition within this glossary.

Abutment: The junction between one building surface and another, as where the roof of one house joins the gable wall of another. Also, in wallpapering, butting one piece of paper up against another.

Adam, James (1732–94): Younger brother of Robert, whom he joined in London, following his own Grand Tour in 1760–3.

Adam, Robert (1728–92): The most famous British architect, furniture designer and decorator of the latter part of the 18th century. His genius emerged after his Grand Tour (1754–8). His subsequent Neo-Classical style was lighter than that of the Palladians who preceded him, or the Greek Revivalists who followed him. The influence of Ancient Rome was strong enough for him to be nicknamed, 'Bob, The Roman'.

Adobe: Brick dried in the sun and used for buildings in Spain, New Mexico and Latin America.

Aesthetic Movement: A late 19th-century movement inspired by the new cult of the Japanese aesthetic and the Queen Anne Revival. It was predominantly a British and American movement with no counterpart in Europe. The emphasis was on maximum light, comfort and informality with pale, pale colours, Japanese symbols, stylized sunflowers, peacocks and lilies.

Andiron: Decorative metal stands in a hearth for supporting logs.

Angle-tie: A timber that joins the wall-plates across the corner of a building with a hipped roof.

Anthemion: Stylized ornament – common in Greek and Roman, Classical and Neo-Classical architecture – based on the leaves and flower of the honeysuckle.

Arabesque: Intricate surface decoration generally based on plant tendrils and leaves, sometimes with the additions of classical vases, sphinxes and so on.

Architrave: The moulded frame surrounding a door or window, or, more specifically, the lowest of the three main parts or mouldings of a classical entablature.

Art Deco: The name given to a style of decorative furniture, furnishings and architecture that flourished in Europe and America from just before World War I until the 1930s. It became increasingly decorative in the 1920s when it blossomed into all sorts of shapes inspired by Aztec, Mayan and African art.

Art Nouveau: Architectural and furnishings style fashionable on both sides of the Atlantic from the 1890s to World War I, known for its sinuous lines and vegetal motifs.

Arts & Crafts Movement: A 19th-century movement, popular on both sides of the Atlantic, that aimed to eschew mass-production methods and return to the individually crafted furnishings of the past. Although it was meant to be an egalitarian movement, its products were too expensive for the masses to buy, although companies like Liberty and Sanderson in the UK have been producing the fabric and wallpaper designs ever since. In the UK it was promulgated by William Morris and C. R. Ashbee. In the United States the movement centred around the Mission style and Prairie school.

Astragal: A small, rounded bead-like moulding that sometimes includes reel- or bobbin-like shapes, when it is then called 'bead and reel'. The term is also used to describe the glazing bars on cabinet doors.

Baluster: Vertical support in stone or wood for a staircase handrail or landing balustrade.

Balustrade: The assembly of handrail, structural post or newel and balusters that flanks a staircase or landing.

Banister: A more commonly used expression for **Baluster**.

Barge board: The boards, often decorated, that are fixed to the incline of a gable wall of a building to hide the ends of the horizontal roof timbers.

Barleysugar twist: Continuous carved twist in a chair leg.

Baroque: Architecture of the 17th and early 18th century in Europe, particularly in Italy, Spain, Germany and Austria, but also France and Britain, based on Classicism but characterized by exuberant decoration and a delight in large-scale masses and vistas. Le Vau, the architect of the Palace of Versailles in France, was a Baroque architect, as were Wren and Vanbrugh in Britain.

Basket grate: A free-standing iron, basket-like grate in which to burn logs and, later, coal.

Bastide: Old French house that was generally fortified.

Bauhaus: A 20th-century German school of design, founded in 1919 by Walter

Gropius, which was an extension of the Weimer School of Arts & Crafts. It was the most powerful single influence in the development and acceptance of modern design. In 1925, the Bauhaus moved from Weimer to Dessau, and the new office building that Gropius designed became a model for the contemporary 'dateless' look that was the epitome of the International style that followed.

Bay window: A window that protrudes from the main wall of a building at ground level with its own side walls and roof.

Beaux Arts: A late 19th-century/early 20th-century classical style favoured by the Ecole des Beaux Arts in Paris, where many of its architectural exponents were trained. The style was much imitated elsewhere.

Belle Epoque: French name for the opulent and glamorous period between the 1890s and World War I when, for the rich, life was supposed to have been better than it had ever been.

Bevel: To cut the edge off a piece of timber or stone so that it slants at either more or less than a 45-degree angle. See also **Chamfer**.

Biedermeier: An Austrian, German and Scandinavian decorative style, known as 'the poor man's Empire', which was popular from the 1820s to the 1840s (and again today). Simple, graceful furniture, like pared-down Empire, was made of mostly golden-hued wood with ebony or black-stained ornamentation.

Boiserie: Panelling decorated with carved or moulded designs in the French style of Louis XIV, XV and XVI.

Bolection moulding: A moulding generally used around wall or door panels, but also some fireplaces. The moulding stands proud of the framing member and is often shaped in a double curve, or ogee.

Bottle glass: Pieces of blown glass discs that have been broken off from the blow pipe during manufacture, now often copied in an attempt to make glass window panes look suitably old.

Bow window: A late 18th- or early 19th-century curved window, used mostly for shops and taverns or inns.

Bracket: A support, often 'S'-shaped and either plain or decorated, for projecting features like shelves or cornices.

Bressumer: Heavy beam used as a massive structural lintel across a wide opening.

Breuer, Marcel (1902–81): Born in Hungary and one of the chief architects and furniture designers of the Bauhaus school, working first with Gropius in Germany until 1931, then London and, after 1937, in the United States, although his independent practice did not really start until after World War II.

Brunelleschi, Filippo (1377–1446): One of the greatest Renaissance architects, less concerned with the revival of antiquity than with practical problems of construction and space management. His masterpiece was the dome of the Cathedral in Florence, begun in 1421.

Bullfinch, Charles (1763–1844): A distinguished late 18th-/early 19th-century American architect from Boston, who produced some of the most dignified public buildings of his time (including the Capitol in Washington D.C.), as well as some elegant terraces of town houses.

Burlington, Richard Boyle, 3rd Earl of (1694–1753): Masterly patron of English Palladianism and a brilliant architect in his own right. He first visited Italy in 1714–15 but did not convert to Palladianism until his return to London. He set out for Italy again to study Palladio's buildings at first hand and returned in 1719 with his protégé William Kent. For the next 30 years he dominated the architectural

scene, spreading the fashion for unadulterated Palladianism.

Cabled fluting: A form of fluting, usually used for pilasters, in which the lower part of each flute is filled with a convex moulding.

Cable moulding: A Romanesque moulding that imitates a twisted cord.

Camber: A surface with a minimal curve, like the soffit, or underside, of an arch.

Cambered collar: A slightly curved horizontal piece of timber joining two principal rafters, like a very shallow arch.

Cambered lintel: A shallow, arched timber, stone or concrete structural component that carries the load over a window or door.

Campbell, Colen (1676–1729): Scottish architect and one of the key figures of Palladianism. He published the first volume of *Vitruvius Britannicus*, based on *De Architectura*, the work of the early Roman architect Vitruvius, which was the principal influence on Renaissance architecture. Campbell remodelled Burlington House for Lord Burlington in 1718–19 and Mereworth Castle in 1722–5, the best of the English versions of Palladio's Rotonda design.

Camp ceiling: An attic-type ceiling that follows the line of the rafters at the sides but is flat across the middle, or a ceiling with an inward curve to suggest a tent.

Cantilever: A projecting beam or slab supported at one end only. Its stability depends upon the amount of loading applied to the tethered end.

Cap: Shortened form of 'capital', used to describe the top of a group of mouldings at the top of a pilaster, column or newel post on a staircase.

Capital: The top part of any column where it spreads to take the load.

It consists of carving or moulding, depending upon its style or period. Also, the top part of a classical pilaster.

Cartouche: A convex lozenge shape, often edged with elaborate moulding to frame some kind of inscription or heraldic figure or figures.

Caryatid: A sculpted female figure used as a column or to support a classical entablature.

Casement: A side-hung window, which opens outwards in Britain and the United States, and inwards in Europe.

Cavetto: A hollow moulding that curves inwards, about a quarter of a circle in section.

Cess-pit: Large underground waterproof storage tank into which drains are run. It is essential that it be pumped out at regular intervals.

Chair rail: A moulded wood or plaster decoration that runs around the walls of a room about a third of the way up – or in any case at the level that might prevent the backs of chairs doing damage to the wall finish.

Chambers, Sir William (1723–96): Famous and influential British 18th-century architect, joint architect with Robert Adam to the King. His style was generally serious and academic, though eclectic enough to produce the famous Chinese Pagoda in Kew Gardens, London, as well as the splendid Somerset House, the façade of which on the Strand is a conscious imitation of a Palladian composition by Inigo Jones.

Chamfer: A symmetrical cut of 45 degrees on beams and lintels, which usually dates from the 17th century or earlier.

Chevron: A zig-zag form of ornament, much used on Norman arches.

Chimney breast: The stone or brick structure projecting into or out of a room and containing the flue.

Chimneypiece: The wood, brick, stone or marble frame surrounding a fireplace, sometimes with an overmantel or mirror above. Also called a mantelpiece.

Chimney shaft: A high chimney with only one flue.

Chimney stack: Masonry or brickwork containing several flues, projecting above the roof and finishing with chimney pots.

Chinoiserie: Chinese motifs like pagodas, cranes, wooden bridges, dragons and exotic birds, highly fashionable in the late 17th and early 18th centuries and the Rococo period.

Cladding: Weatherproofing or decorative surface fixed to a structural element of a wall, such as slates, weatherboarding (clapboard) and tiles.

Clapboard: US term for weatherboarding or cladding on houses, put up for protection from the weather.

Classical architecture or Classicism: A style either imitating or inspired by Ancient Greece or Rome or the classical trend in 16th-century Renaissance Italy. Various forms of Classicism have woven in and out of the centuries ever since. It is characterized by symmetry and balance, geometrical forms, clean lines, and classical architectural details like columns, pilasters and pediments.

Classical orders: The five styles of Ancient architecture – Tuscan, Doric, Ionic, Corinthian and Composite – based on the proportions and decoration of different types of column. The simplest order is Tuscan, although the Doric dates from an earlier time. The Ionic is more decorative, the Corinthian highly ornamental. The Composite order combines features from the Ionic and Corinthian orders.

Clerestory window: Window placed near the ceiling of a high room or hall in order to receive light from above the roofs of neighbouring buildings. Also, a window piercing the upper storey of the nave of a church.

Closed-string staircase: 'Strings' are actually the main framing members forming the sides of a staircase. Closed-string varieties have their treads housed in the strings, as opposed to an 'open-string' staircase, where the shape of the stairs is cut out with the treads resting on the string. 'Wall-string' stairs are fixed to the wall of the stairwell.

Coade stone: Artificial stone invented by a Mrs Eleanor Coade in the 1770s, and later marketed by Coade and Sealy of London. It was very widely used in the late 18th and 19th centuries for all types of ornamentation.

Collar beams: A tension timber that runs horizontally between the principal rafters of a roof truss. Usually, it has the same thickness as the principal rafters and is mortise-and-tenoned into them.

Collar purlin: A roof timber that runs below the centre of every collar in a series of trusses. It is usually supported in its turn by crown posts.

Collars: Horizontal timbers spiked to each pair of rafters in a roof to check any tendency for the ends of the rafters to pull apart under the weight of the load. Attic ceilings are often fixed to them.

Colonial style: A style originally developed by Europeans in their colonies but especially applied to, initially, the southern states of America with adapted Renaissance and Neo-Classical elements, combined and developed according to personal taste. It was then applied to the most popular vernacular style of architecture all over the United States. 18th- and 19th-century European Colonial evokes verandas, white-painted weatherboarding, or clapboard, handsome porticoes and pillars, green- or white-painted shutters, bare polished floorboards, rattan furniture and large swooshing ceiling fans. American Colonial covers, first, the late 16th/early 17th century, which was more a period of making do with imported furniture or more primitive local work and plain, sturdy houses, and the lovely late 18th-century houses and furniture achieved when the Federal Government was established. American Colonial is associated with the same white clapboard and shutters, charming porticoes, painted floors and some of the most beautiful 18th- and 19th-century domestic architecture and furniture that exists.

Column: Vertical, rounded support for an entablature or arch, varying in shape according to the style or classical order. In fact, the shape of columns is a major factor in determining classical styles.

Commonwealth style: Severely plain style of architecture favoured in Cromwellian times in Britain and much used by the first American settlers on the East Coast.

Composite order: Classical Roman order that combines the Ionic capital with the Corinthian one.

Coping: A course of quite substantial stones that usually tops a parapet or upstanding gable walls.

Corbel: A stone or timber support that projects from a wall to carry the load of a structural member like a beam.

Corinthian order: Classical order of architecture (along with Tuscan, Doric, Ionic and Composite) with column capitals freely decorated with acanthus leaves. It is the most elaborately decorated of the five orders and was a 5th-century BC Greek invention, later developed by the Romans, who, in turn, provided the prototype for the Renaissance form.

Cornice: The top of the three parts of a classical entablature, composed of several different mouldings, usually with a 'fillet' and 'cyma recta' (like an assymetrical flattened-out 'S' with the hollow curve uppermost). Also the decorative moulding that runs around a room between ceiling and wall, or any projecting ornamental moulding along the top of a building, wall or arch, 'finishing' or 'crowning' it.

Cortile: Italian word for a courtyard, usually internal and often surrounded by arcades.

Cottage orné: An artificial or deliberately rustic building often with a thatched roof and weatherboarding, or clapboard, and roughly hewn wooden columns. Such buildings, mostly used for park lodges or agricultural buildings, were products of the Picturesque style of the late 18th and early 19th centuries in Britain and in the United States.

Counter battens: Slim fillets of wood nailed to battens running in the opposite direction to provide adequate fixing points for boards, plasterboard, wallboarding or laths.

Cove: Substantial concave moulding used like a cornice to join ceilings to walls.

Crown glass: Glass blown into a disc and then cut out to form crown-glass window panes – the main method for making window lights until the 1830s.

Crown post: Many early roofs had trusses consisting of rafters joined by tie beams from which crown posts supported collar purlins running under the middle of the collars. Examining old roof beams is a fairly fail-safe way of dating a house.

Crucks: Pairs of stout curved timbers with a branched effect used as the principal framing of a house. They can take the place of both posts for the walls and rafters for the roof.

Curtail step: The bottom step of a staircase that is projected sideways and curled around like a dog's or 'cur's' tail.

Cusp: Gothic tracery usually took the form of trefoil or quatrefoil ornament. A quatrefoil is composed of four curves and at the point where they join they form 'cusps'.

Cyma recta: Moulding with a double 'S'-shaped curve, concave above and convex below, also known as an ogee moulding.

Cyma reversa: Like cyma recta but convex above and concave below. It is also known as a reverse ogee moulding.

Dado: Wood (or otherwise simulated) panelling running around the lower part of a room from skirting, or base board, to waist height. In classical terms it is the portion of a plinth or pedestal between the base and the cornice.

Damp-proof course: A layer of impervious material built into the thickness of a wall to prevent moisture rising from the ground into the fabric of the main structure.

Damp-proof membrane: Usually a layer of plastic sheeting used in restoration work for damp-proofing.

Demi-lune: Half-moon or elliptically shaped window.

Dentil: A small, square (tooth-shaped) block moulding used in series in Ionic, Corinthian, Composite and, occasionally, Doric cornices. Also used on its own.

De Stijl: Name of a group of avant-garde Dutch designers in the 1920s who worked mainly in right angles and primary colours. Members included the architect and designer Gerrit Rietveld and the painter Piet Mondrian.

Directoire: The style current in France in the last five years of the 18th century,

between the assassination of Louis XVI and the coup d'état of Napoleon Bonaparte. In fact it was little different from the simple and elegant Louis Seize style with somewhat inferior materials.

Distress: To age a material artificially, whether by scoring, denting, chipping, staining, or by *faux* painting methods.

Dog grate: A free-standing iron or steel basket grate dating from the 18th century with a cast-iron fire back and pronounced front legs.

Dog-leg staircase: Two flights of stairs in which the first flight ends at a half-landing and the stairs then double back in a second flight to the landing itself. The outer string of the second flight is directly, or very nearly directly, above the first.

Doorcase: All the joinery work that frames, surrounds or adorns a door.

Doorhood: A projecting roof-like feature supported on brackets that gives both visual emphasis to a door and shelter for those gaining access.

Doric order: One of the classical orders of architecture (the others being Tuscan, Ionic, Corinthian and Composite). The simplest columnar shape is the Tuscan,

although the Doric is considered to be earlier and is divided between the Greek and Roman Doric. The former has no base, as seen on the Parthenon and the temples at Paestum in southern Italy.

Dormer window: A window that protrudes from the slope of a roof with its own miniature roofing structure.

Dovetail nailing: Nails are hammered through one piece of wood to another at opposite angles to make it difficult to pull the timbers apart.

Down-hearth: A fireplace where the fire is laid on the actual hearthstone, sometimes with the help of firedogs.

Dubbing-out: Filling major cavities, depressions and other scars in a wall with mortar before applying the first coat of plaster.

Duck: Tough linen and cotton mix fabric used for upholstery.

Duck's nest grate: A basic, low-hob grate that can rest on firedogs or be self-sufficient; originally used mostly for 18th- and early 19th-century kitchens.

Eaves: The edges of a roof sticking out beyond a wall.

Edwardian: Called after Edward VII and more or less the same period in Britain and the United States as the Belle Epoque in France (between the 1890s and World War I). Designs were much lighter and airier than the Victorian decoration and building that had gone before. The period also encompasses the Aesthetic Movement, Arts & Crafts, Art Nouveau and the Queen Anne Revival, which was sometimes known as the time of 'sweetness and light'.

Egg-and-dart moulding: A row of egg-shaped ornaments generally divided up by small arrow or tongue motifs. It is often used to embellish small convex mouldings.

Elevation: The façade and general exterior walls of a building.

Elizabethan: The Elizabethan period was during the reign of Elizabeth I in the second half of the 16th century. The period was one of great prosperity, so there was an increased demand for more domestic architecture and furnishings, and new houses (many of them still standing proudly) were built up and down the country. The style was largely based on Italian Renaissance forms as translated by the French and Flemish, united to the last of the late Gothic with its emphasis on very large windows with mullions and transoms, plus the adoption of the Netherlands fashion for strapwork for ceilings, making the style somewhat idiosyncratic with much carving and inlay. Houses were often 'E'- or 'H'-shaped, and gables, either straight or curved, as in the Netherlands, were frequent. Brick was used as well as half timbering, and houses had dominant chimney stacks. Inside, small wood panels were combined with pilasters and columns. In low-ceilinged rooms the panelling rose from the skirtings, or base boards, to a primitive cornice. In grander houses, an oak dado was surmounted by a moulding, then panelling and finally an entablature.

Ell: American single-storey lean-to wing containing a kitchen, generally added in the 17th century to clapboard, timber-framed New England houses.

Embrasure: A recess for a window, door or a small opening in a wall, usually splayed on the inside.

Empire: Early 19th-century style during the reign of Napoleon in France (1804–15) and a little later in the United States. Designs were partly derived from the Neo-Classical with an emphasis on Imperial Rome; partly on Egyptian details brought back by Napoleon from the Egyptian Campaigns; and partly on the discoveries of the ruins at Pompeii and Herculaneum in Italy. In the United States the American bald eagle also began to be incorporated as a regular motif.

Encaustic tiles: Patterned earthenware tiles, often glazed, and greatly favoured by Victorian and Edwardian builders.

Enfilade: Axial arrangement of doorways connecting a suite of rooms so that one obtains a vista down the whole length of the suite.

Entablature: The topmost horizontal element of a classical order, or column consisting of architrave, frieze and cornice.

Escutcheon: The ornamental and protective plate that surrounds the keyhole of a door.

Facing: The finish applied to the outer surface of a building.

Fanlight: The glazed light above a door in 18th- and early 19th-century buildings, often semi-circular or fan-shaped with radiating glazing bars or other ornamentation. Sometimes the term is used erroneously for rectangular lights above doors, which are more correctly called transoms.

Fascia: A plain horizontal band in a classical architrave or a board that runs horizontally under the eaves of a building to which the guttering can be attached.

Federal: American architecture and design from the 1780s until the early 19th century and based on Neo-Classicism. It drew on early Regency architecture in Britain and early Empire in France but regurgitated them all in a uniquely elegant American way.

Fielded panel: A wall or door panel with a raised centre area that is bevelled or sloped off or 'fielded' around the sides.

Fillets: Plain narrow bands of wood, stone or plaster that divide more complicated mouldings from each other.

Finial: A formal turned or carved ornament in the shape of an urn, ball, bun, spike, arrow, fleur de lys or figure at the top of a gable, canopy, pinnacle, newel post on a stairway or at either end of a curtain pole.

Fireback: A cast-iron slab with an ornamental design that stands at the back of a fireplace to protect the wall and help reflect heat. Long, low shapes are probably 16th century; the more upright they are, the later they are.

Firedogs: Smaller than andirons, they are three-legged with an upstand at the front end and are used to hold logs while they burn.

Fire-hood: A canopy in metal, plaster, brick or stone to stand right over the fire on a big open hearth to channel smoke into the flue of a chimney.

Flashings: Strips of waterproof material used to make watertight the abutments between slates and chimneys, walls and roofs, walls and windows and so on.

Flush door: Plain, smooth door, either solid or hollow core, surfaced with plywood or a laminate.

Fluting: Shallow concave grooves running vertically on the shaft of a column, pilaster or other surface. If the lower part is filled with a solid cylindrical piece, it is called cabled fluting.

French windows: Pairs of narrow, glazed doors giving access to the outside or another room or hallway. They generally open inwards, as do windows in France from which their name derives. (Interestingly, such windows in France are called *fenêtres anglaises*.)

Fret: Also known as fretwork, this is pierced decoration that generally takes the form of a repeated motif on a gallery around a table top or on chair legs or stretchers. See also **Greek key pattern** and **Key pattern**.

Frieze: The decorative band along the upper part of an internal wall or the middle division of an entablature between the architrave and cornice.

Gable: The triangular upper portion of a wall between the sloping ends of a pitched roof.

Gazebo: Either the turret on the roof of an open ornamental garden summerhouse, or the whole structure.

Georgian: The term applied to British architecture and design during the reigns of George I, II, III and IV, a long period from 1714 to 1830 that was divided into early, mid-, late Georgian and Regency and went from Palladianism to Neo-Classicism. Sometimes called 'the Age of Elegance', it was certainly the golden age of British design in every field.

Gesso: This is made from gypsum or chalk with glue to bind it to form a dense white base for the decoration of panelling or for gilded mouldings.

Gibbons, Grinling (1648–1721): Dutch immigrant to Britain and great Restoration carver of wood (and plaster) in the 17th century, who achieved new heights of technical skill. Horace Walpole described his wonderful musical instruments (carved entirely in the round) in the Carved Room at Petworth House, Sussex 'as worthy of the Grecian age of Cameos'. He also carved the choir stalls at Saint Paul's Cathedral, London, but these were only a few of his many major works.

Gilding: Gold or other metallic leaf is applied like a transfer to a surface coated with sticky gold-size or a weak glue.

Girandole: 17th-century word (derived from the Italian) for wall light (in France 'a cluster of diamonds' or chandelier). By the mid-18th century it had come to describe the combination of carved wood and mirror plate plus candles of the Rococo, then the more restrained wall mirrors with candle branches of the Neo-Classical era.

Glazing bars: The wooden framing members in a sash window that divide and contain the glass panes. Early bars, that is to say late 17th century and Queen Anne period, were wide, flat and fairly crude. They became progressively finer and more subtly moulded in the 18th century. Early 19th-century bars were very slender.

Gothic: Medieval architectural and particularly ecclesiastical style from approximately 1200 to 1500, typified by the use of the pointed arch. Like Classicism, it is one of the great influences weaving in and out of other centuries and styles. Much 16th- and 17th-century work is Gothic in some detail or other. Gothic Revival started around 1750; then came Regency Gothic in the early 19th century, often known as 'Gothick', and finally Victorian Gothic, which surfaced in the 1840s. Pugin's Houses of Parliament in London are a fine example of Victorian Gothic, as are many municipal American and European buildings.

Graining: The practice of painting and staining softwoods to make them look like various hardwoods with interesting figuring. This was often practised in the late 17th century as well as the Victorian and Edwardian eras, and it is currently favoured again.

Grand Tour: An almost obligatory part of education for rich young 18th-century European men, particularly the British, who flocked to Italy and Greece and, to a lesser extent, to France, to steep themselves in classical antiquity. After two or three years they returned laden

with ancient treasures and new ideas for building splendid homes or improving old ones.

Greek key pattern: Horizontal pattern of interwoven horizontal and vertical lines. See also **Fret** and **Key pattern**.

Greek Revival: Late 18th-/early 19th-century style of architecture that embraced classical Greek models rather than Renaissance Roman forms. It was at its height in Britain and France in the 1790s and early 1800s and became enormously popular in the United States from around 1820 to 1840, becoming practically de rigueur for official buildings as well as handsome houses.

Grip floor: Mixture of beaten lime and ash, normally used on the ground floor in some early 16th-, 17th- and 18th-century houses, but occasionally upstairs when it was placed on top of laths supported by joists.

Grip handrail: Heavy Elizabethan or Jacobean handrail on stairs with a pronounced roll moulding on top.

Gropius, Walter (1883–1969): Founder of the Bauhaus School in Weimar, Germany and one of the great pioneers of the International style. He left Germany for Britain when Hitler assumed power. He then left Britain for Harvard in 1937.

Grotesque: Fanciful ornamental decoration in the form of heads, sphinxes, medallions, etc, carved in stucco or stone and used by early Romans on the walls of buildings. When they were rediscovered, they were underground (i.e., in grottoes), hence the name, which, in fact, has nothing whatsoever to do with the odd, ugly meaning we now give to the word.

Grout: Cement and sand mixture (mostly cement and a little sand) used for fixing tiles, bricks and stones.

Gustavian: Charming, late 18th-century Swedish Neo-Classical style named after Gustav III (1771–1792) who made the Swedish court a northern Versailles. The style is typified by grey-blue-painted furniture, simple checks and stripes, straw yellows, muted pinks, clear blues, pearl greys and splendid tiled stoves.

Hardouin-Mansart, Jules (1646–1708): Although not to be confused with his great uncle François Mansart of mansard roof fame, he created the splendid Gallerie des Glaces at Versailles and became Louis XIV's court architect. He was also in charge of the vast extensions of Versailles, built the Trianon and Orangerie and planned the Place Vendôme (from 1698).

Header: A brick that appears head-on on the face of a wall. See also **Stretcher**.

Herms: Three-quarter-length figures on pedestals used decoratively from the Renaissance onwards. See also **Terms**.

Herringbone work: Stone, brick or tile work in which the components are laid diagonally instead of horizontally. Alternate courses lie in opposite directions, forming a zig-zag design.

Hipped roof: Roof with sloped rather than vertical ends.

Hip rafter: A diagonally placed rafter at the external junction between roof slopes. Internal junctions are called valleys.

Hips: The external junctions between roof slopes.

Hob grate: Cast-iron coal-burning grate made from the late 18th century onwards.

Hood-mould: A projecting moulding to throw off the rain on the face of a wall above an early arch, doorway or window.

Inglenook fireplace: A large open fireplace with a down-hearth and a built-in seat or seats inside the chimney

breast. It first appeared in the 16th century and was commonly used in the 17th century as well as in rural houses in the early 18th century.

Inlaid floor: A kind of parquet floor, sometimes described as a marquetry floor, with wood strips laid with and against the grain. The decoration is seldom truly inlaid into the actual carcass timber.

Intaglio: An engraved design in stone that gives a relief image when pressed into wax.

Intarsia: A form of mosaic made up of different coloured woods, which was popular in 15th- and 16th-century Italy, especially for the floors of libraries, studies, small ante rooms in palaces and the choirs in churches.

Interlocking tiles: Tiles designed so that their edges fit together to provide a weatherproof seal.

International style: Architectural style, characterized by rectilinear shapes and the use of steel, glass and reinforced concrete, created before World War I by such architects as Gropius and Wright. Also known as Modernism.

Intrados: The inner curve or underside of an arch. Also called a **Soffit**.

Ionic order: One of the classical orders (together with Tuscan, Doric, Corinthian and Composite). It originated in Asia Minor in the mid-6th century BC and has deep volutes or spiral scrolls at the column head but no accompanying acanthus leaves.

Jacobean architecture: Leading on from Elizabethan architecture, this English Renaissance style of the 17th century has a mixture of elaborate decoration, Gothic touches and often rather crude attempts at the Classical order. As in Elizabethan architecture, there are many fine examples of it extant – mellow red brick, stone quoins, hipped roofs, dormer windows and gables.

Jambs: The sides of a door opening, or just an opening, whether made of stone, brick or wood.

Jib door: A disguised door fitted within a wall, or panelling, or *faux* bookshelves, and appearing to be part of the whole.

Joinery: The final finished woodwork in a house such as doors, trims, stairs, panelling, skirtings, or base boards. Also the fitting and making of such items.

Jones, Inigo (1573–1652): Amazingly avant-garde designer and architect, who imported Classical style from Italy – which he first visited in 1603 – and brought the English Renaissance to maturity. He visited Italy again in 1613 and stayed for a year and a quarter, studying Palladio's designs and Ancient Roman monuments. His Palladian-inspired designs back in Britain, however, were far from mere copies, for the details were all subtly transmuted. Famous buildings by Jones that are still very much standing include The Queen's House, Greenwich; his great Corinthian portico for Saint Paul's Cathedral, London; Wilton House, Wiltshire (with his assistant Isaac de Caus, finished by his pupil and nephew by marriage John Webb); and the church and fragment of a square (the rest has been rebuilt), in Covent Garden, London, thought to have been inspired by the Place des Vosges in Paris.

Kent, William (1685–1748): Great British architect, furniture designer and landscape designer. The protégé of Lord Burlington, he was apparently as happy designing Gothic buildings as Palladian, although his patron guided him along strict classical lines in his major commissions. His furniture and interior decoration were sumptuous: richly carved and gilded and derived partly from Italian Baroque and partly

from Inigo Jones, whose designs he edited and published in 1727. He did not actually take up architecture until he was in his 40s. Kent masterpieces include Holkham Hall in Norfolk, and, in London, the Horse Guards, The Treasury, 17 Arlington Street and 44 Berkeley Square. He was also the virtual creator of British landscape gardening, having seen 'that all nature is a garden'. From his time onwards country houses were designed to harmonize with the landscape rather than to dominate and control it.

Key pattern: A geometrical ornament of both horizontal and vertical straight lines. See also **Fret** and **Greek key pattern**.

Keystone: The central stone – sometimes carved – of an arch or rib vault.

King post: The middle upright post in a roof truss connecting the tie or collar beam with the roof ridge.

Knapped flint: Flint split in two so that the smooth black surfaces of the split sides form the facing on a wall.

Lath: Thin narrow strips of wood used to provide a supporting framework for plaster, tiles, etc.

Le Corbusier (1887–1966): One of the most influential architects of the 20th century was born Charles-Edouard Jeanneret in Switzerland. His main interests were the mass-production of housing (The Unité d'Habitation at Marseilles,1947–52); city and town planning (Ville Contemporaine, 1922; Plain Voisin, 1925; Ville Radieuse,1935 and Plan for Algiers, 1930); and new types of private housing, white, cubist and with rooms flowing into each other like his villas at Garches (1927) and Poissy (1929–31). He laid out the town and built the law courts and secretariat at Chandigarh in India, which had a particularly strong influence in Japan. As a result, Corbusier went on to design the Museum of Modern Art in Tokyo.

Le Vau, Louis (1612–70): The leading Baroque architect in France, but less intellectual than his contemporary Jules Hardouin-Mansart. He headed a splendid group of decorators, sculptors, painters, wood carvers and gardeners with which he helped to create the Louis XIV style at Versailles, which he entirely remodelled before Hardouin-Mansart ruined it with alterations and extensions. Previously, he was commissioned by the King's first minister, Fouquet, to design his country house at Vaux-le-Vicomte, which le Vau turned into the most splendid of all French chateaux in only a year of building.

Lights: Nothing to do with lighting but the professional term for window glass.

Linenfold panelling: Panelling carved to look like stylized folds of fabric, usually 16th-century Tudor.

Lintel: Structural component, usually of wood, stone, or concrete, that carries the load over a window, door or fireplace opening.

Listed building: In the United Kingdom, this is a building listed by the Department of the Environment as being of particular architectural or historical interest. There are three grades (I, II and III) in that order of importance. Such buildings are protected by law inside and out against unauthorized demolition and any work that could destroy the building's character. Equivalent listings exist in both Europe and the United States.

Loggia: The covered area on the side of a building.

Lozenge panelling: Diamond-shaped decoration in Jacobean panelling.

Mackintosh, Charles Rennie (1868–1928): One of the few British Art Nouveau architects, and the greatest. He studied at the Glasgow School of

Art, and in 1896 won the competition to design the new building of the School, which he achieved in a uniquely harmonious way, combining the crisply rectangular with the languid curves of Art Nouveau. His furnishings made a deep impression on the Austrian architects of the Wiener Werkstätte when Mackintosh exhibited some of his work at the Vienna Secession in 1900. The Viennese were in the process of abandoning Art Nouveau for cleaner, straighter lines, as practised by Josef Hoffman and Adolf Loos, just as Mackintosh was showing his unique white lacquered chairs and cupboards with gentle inlays of metal with pink, mauve or mother-of-pearl enamel.

Manor house: A large house in the country or the largest house in a village, called a *manoir* in France. Architecturally, the term is used to denote an unfortified, medium-sized house from the late Middle Ages.

Mansard: The roof named after François Mansart's roof at Blois, with a double slope, the lower being longer and steeper than the upper.

Mansart, François (1598–1666): Great French classical architect. One of his masterpieces was the Orléans wing of the Chateau de Blois (1635–8), where he introduced the continuous broken roof with a steep lower slope and flatter, shorter upper portion that is named after him. See also **Mansard**.

Mast newel staircase: Spiral staircase with timber treads housed in a central post that rises up through the building or through an attached turret or wing.

Matchboarding: Thin softwood boards used particularly in the United States for lining rooms, sometimes with an edge bead.

Medallion: In building, decorative oval or circle often containing a plaster head or figure in relief or a painting.

Mies van der Rohe, Ludwig (1886–1969): One of the great Bauhaus architects who became caught up in World War I with the enthusiasm of Expressionism and designed his first revolutionary glass skyscrapers (1919–21). But his true talent was first revealed in the German Pavilion for the Barcelona Exhibition in 1929 with its masterly spatial composition and immaculate and precious finishes. He directed the Bauhaus from 1930–3 but moved to America where, in 1938, he was made Professor of Architecture at what is now The Institute of Technology in Chicago. One of his most famous New York buildings is the Seagram Building on Park Avenue.

Mission style: This architectural style began in California and spread throughout the American Southwest. Celebrating the architecture of Hispanic settlers, Mission style houses feature arched dormers and roof parapets. Some resemble old Spanish mission churches with twin bell towers and elaborate arches. By the 1920s, architects were combining Mission styling with features from the craftsman and Prairie movements.

Mitre: At corners, architraves and moldings are sawn to butt together at a 45-degree angle.

Modernism: See **International style**.

Morris, William (1834–96): Although not an architect himself, he had an enormous influence on the design profession in general. He studied all things medieval at Oxford with his friend Edward Burne-Jones, the Pre-Raphaelite painter, who introduced him to other Pre-Raphaelites. He became inspired by the idea of the intrinsic value of craftsmanship, as well as a firm believer in the importance of beautiful surroundings for the creation of human happiness. Appalled at the effects of mass-production, he started his firm of Morris, Marshall, Faulkner & Co. in 1861. His first product was a cabinet designed

by Philip Webb, the architect of his famous Red House made of unadorned red brick, with windows by Burne-Jones and furniture designed by Webb, Morris and Burne-Jones as well. Morris painted this cabinet with inspiration from the Renaissance collection in the Victoria and Albert Museum, where the cabinet now resides. He went on to make good solid furniture and to design wallpapers and fabrics using vegetable dyes and traditional methods of manufacture. This unified approach to interior decoration was the start of the Arts & Crafts Movement. Alas, the historic handwork methods used to produce his goods proved disastrously expensive, although his paper and fabric designs are still much in evidence and made by Liberty and Sanderson. 'Whatever you have in your room,' said Morris, 'think first of your walls, for they are that which makes your house a home.' Not bad advice.

Mortar: Generally a mixture of cement and sand, although sometimes lime as well or lime and sand, and used to fix bricks or stones together.

Mortise: A slot or recess cut into a piece of wood, stone, etc, designed to receive a matching projecting piece (tenon).

Mouldings: Shaped lengths of wood, plaster or stone used as ornament in a room or on furniture, or used to conceal joints between one building surface and another.

Muff glass: Early glass used for window panes. Muff or cylinder glass was blown in a cylinder form, then slit lengthwise and unrolled into flat pieces from which the panes were cut.

Mullions: Timber or stone uprights that divided windows vertically into 'lights'.

Muntins: Intermediate uprights framing members in doors or windows.

Nash, John (1752–1835): Considered to be the only inspired town planner of London – the layout of Regent Street and Regent's Park in London (1811 onwards), and Trafalgar Square, Clarence House, Carlton House Terrace, Suffolk Street, All Soul's, Langham Place, all planned in the 1820s, and Buckingham Palace. He was dismissed from Buckingham Palace, though, when his patron George IV died in 1830 (the palace was completed by Edward Blore, a comparative unknown). Nash was the great architect of the Picturesque Movement and the first to introduce stucco-fronted houses.

Neo-Classicism: The first really international style, popular all over the western world and the Antipodes from the latter part of the 18th century to the first quarter of the 19th. It was based on Ancient Greek and Roman forms as noted by visiting architects, and became increasingly popular after the discovery of the ruins at Paestum, Herculaneum and Pompeii.

Newel: A structural post in stone, wood or metal to support a balustrade at the top and bottom and at any change of direction in the staircase.

Newel stair: A spiral staircase made of wood or stone.

Niche: A recess in a wall, often with an arched top, for a statue, piece of sculpture or bust.

Nogging: Short lengths of wood that are fixed between the vertical studs of a partition to strengthen the construction. In old timber-framed houses the spaces between posts are filled with bricks called 'brick nogging'.

Norman architecture: The architecture of the Norman Conquest (1066) in England until the beginning of the Gothic style, sometimes linked with Romanesque architecture, as in the rib-vaulting of Durham Cathedral. The style first emerged with the rebuilding of Westminster Abbey by Edward the Confessor around 1045 onwards as a continuation of the style that was used for Mont Saint Michel and the churches of Caen in Normandy. Externally there were two façade towers and a square crossing tower, a design used for Canterbury and Southwell cathedrals as well. Inside, there was an arcade, a gallery with large or sub-divided openings towards the nave. The Normans rebuilt nearly every cathedral and abbey church in England.

Nosing: The part of a stair tread that sticks out above the riser.

Obelisk: A tall, tapering shaft of stone like granite or marble of square or rectangular section and ending like a pyramid. Greatly used in Ancient Egypt.

Oculus: A round window.

Oeil-de-boeuf **window:** A small, circular window.

Ogee moulding: An 'S'-shaped section like cyma recta or cyma reversa.

Open-well stairs: A staircase rising in relatively short flights to quarter-landings, built around an open well. It was first used in the 16th century.

Oriel window: A projecting window on an upper floor supported by a corbel or bracket.

Ormolu: An alloy of copper, zinc and tin made to resemble gold and used mostly for furniture decorating.

Overmantel: The upper part of a chimneypiece above the mantelpiece shelf. It is usually a panel topped by a cornice or pediment. Sometimes it also comprises a mirror and shelves.

Ovolo: A small convex moulding.

Pagoda: A Buddhist temple in the form of a polygonal tower, with elaborately ornamented roofs projecting from each of its many storeys. Common in China and India and seen in Chinoiserie in the West.

Palisade: A fence made of iron or wooden stakes.

Palladian style: Based upon Andreo Palladio's architecture in 16th-century Renaissance Italy and very influential on English 17th- and 18th-century architecture. Inigo Jones first introduced the style to Britain on his return from Italy in 1614, but the great Palladian revival began both in Italy and Britain in the early 18th century, where it was led by Colen Campbell and Lord Burlington.

Palladio, Andrea (1508–80): One of the greatest and certainly the most influential of Italian architects. He distilled various Renaissance ideas, particularly the revival of Ancient Roman symmetrical planning and 'harmonic' proportions. He aimed to recapture the splendour of antiquity but he was also influenced by such predecessors as Michelangelo and Raphael and, to some extent, by the Byzantine architecture of Venice. In the 1550s he evolved a formula for the

'ideal' villa, a central block of a severely symmetrical plan, decorated outside with a portico and continued by long wings of farm buildings, either extended horizontally or curved forwards in quadrants. He employed numerous variations on this theme, from the more elaborate La Rotonda (begun in 1550), with its porticos on each of its four sides, to the extreme simplicity of La Malcontenta (1560), and the stark severity of Poiana where columns are replaced by undecorated shafts.

Palmette: A fan-shaped ornament composed of narrow divisions like a palm leaf. It is a frequent Neo-Classical motif.

Pantile: Interlocking 'S'-shaped roof tile.

Parapet: A low, sometimes battlemented wall, placed to protect anywhere there is a sudden drop, i.e., at the top of a flat roof or on the edge of a bridge or quay.

Pargetting: Ornamental exterior plasterwork in relief or intaglio in vine patterns, other foliage or figures. It is most often found in timber-framed buildings in eastern England.

Parquet floor: Wood floor made up of thin hardwood blocks, about 5mm (¼in) thick and often arranged in herringbone or squared patterns on a wood sub-floor, then highly polished.

Patera: Small disc-like oval or circular ornament in classical architecture that was a particular favourite of Neo-Classical architects like Robert Adam. It is often decorated with acanthus leaves or rose petals and used on fireplaces or decorative plaster friezes.

Patio: In Spanish or Spanish American architecture it is an inner courtyard open to the sky, but it has become a generic English word for an outside paved or bricked area.

Pavilion: A lightly constructed ornamental building often used as a summerhouse, or

'pleasurehouse', in a garden, or attached to a cricket or other sports ground.

Pebbledash: Small rounded stones like pea gravel, dashed into cement and plaster before it has set to achieve a densely textured wall finish. Also called **Roughcast**.

Pedestal: The base supporting a column in classical architecture, or the base for a statue, bust or piece of sculpture.

Pediment: A triangular or segmented feature in wood, stone or plaster that forms the topmost element of a classical door, window, fireplace or large piece of furniture like a bureau-bookcase. A broken pediment has a gap at the top of the triangle.

Pele-tower: Northern English or Scottish term for a small fortified house or tower formerly ready for sudden defence.

Pentice: A roof with post, pillar or pier supports covering an outside staircase. Also a gallery with its own roof.

Pergola: A covered garden walkway or paved area outside a house, formed of upright posts or pillars and horizontal beams. Can be made of wood or stone.

Picturesque movement: The early 19th-century style defined in the 18th century as an aesthetic quality between the sublime and the beautiful. It was characterized in gardening by wild ruggedness with rushing streams, waterfalls, apparently impenetrable woods and so on. In architecture it was characterized by assymetrical forms, Gothic and Italianate country houses and *cottages ornés*. John Nash was a particular proponent of the Picturesque.

Pier: A solid masonry support as opposed to a column, or the solid mass between windows or doors in a building.

Pilaster: A flat, rectangular version of a column attached to a wall, more for decoration than structure. Often used as the side pieces for a pair of columns supporting a squared arch.

Pillar: A free-standing upright that, unlike a column, does not have to be cylindrical or conform to any of the Classical orders.

Plinth: The base of a column or pedestal, generally chamfered or moulded at the top.

Podium: A continuous base or plinth supporting columns, or the platform enclosing the arena in an Ancient Roman amphitheatre, still used as a stand for making speeches.

Pointing: The mortar filling between bricks or stones in a wall.

Porch: The covered entrance to a building (UK), called a portico if columned and pedimented like a temple front; a covered veranda (US).

Portcullis: An iron gate or iron-reinforced wooden bars that slides up and down in vertical grooves in the jambs of a doorway. Used for the defence of castles and fortified houses.

Porte-cochere: A porch that is big enough for cars and, formerly, carriages to pass under.

Portico: A roofed space, either open or partly enclosed, forming the entrance and centrepiece of the façade of a house, church or temple. It often has detached or attached columns and a pediment.

Postern: A small gateway that is sometimes deliberately concealed at the back of a castle, monastery or even a walled town (as in postern gate).

Prairie school: The Prairie style was developed in the late 19th and early 20th centuries by Frank Lloyd Wright and other architects as 'a modern architecture for a democratic American society'. Common characteristics are horizontal proportions,

flat brick or stucco walls, often outlined with wooden strips of contrasting colour, windows with abstract, geometric ornament, and hip or gable roofs with wide overhanging eaves.

Profile: In architecture and building, the section of a moulding, or the contour or outline of a building, or part of it.

Prostyle: Free-standing columns in a row, as in a portico.

Pugin, Augustus Welby (1812–52): One of the great Victorian Gothic architects. He designed furniture for Windsor Castle before he was 20 and designed the façades of the Houses of Parliament, as well as such Gothic details as the hat racks and ink stands inside.

Purlins: Square-section timbers running lengthwise along the roof and resting on the principal rafters as they carry the lighter and more numerous 'common rafters'.

Putti: Italian cherubs much used in Baroque and Rococo art and architecture.

Quadrant mould: Moulding of a quarter-circle section.

Quarry tiles: Unglazed, non-porous, burnt clay tiles that are usually red.

Queen Anne Revival: Style started around 1860 by the architect Richard Norman Shaw and others who were interested in English vernacular architecture, building houses with traditional English materials: red brick, white-painted woodwork and sash windows in the style of Wren. Interiors were planned to give the effect of an old house with inglenooks, odd little rooms called 'snugs', bay windows with window seats, steps up and down from rooms and a great deal more light. Hence the epithet 'sweetness and light'. This style was also popular in America and it continued through the Edwardian period until the advent of World War I.

Queen Anne style: Baroque architecture in the time of Queen Anne carried on from the semi-Dutch style of William and Mary. Vanbrugh (Castle Howard and Blenheim) was one of the grand architects of the time, but on the domestic front the so-called 'Wren' house persisted (Wren did not actually design any houses) in their mellow red brick. The style was very popular in America where it continued long after the death of the monarch.

Quoins: Squared-up or 'dressed' stones that form the corners of a building.

Rafters: Common rafters carry the battens or laths from which roof tiles or slates are slung.

Rebate: A step-shaped recess cut from a piece of timber as in a picture frame to take the glass.

Reeding: Closely (but sometimes widely) spaced half-round beading often used in 19th-century architraves and furniture legs.

Register grate: Cast-iron or sheet-metal plate fills the main fireplace opening with a diminished opening for quite a small fitted grate. It was popular during the second half of the 19th century, particularly for bedrooms and smaller rooms.

Rendering: The first coat of plaster on a solid wall and sometimes the only coat.

Return: When a wall or moulding changes direction at right angles.

Reveal: The visible exterior parts of a window jamb or door between the frame and the main wall surface.

Ribs: Elizabethan and Jacobean plasterwork usually made up of 'ribbed' designs. Also means the structural 'ribs' used in vaulting.

Ridge: The apex of a pitched roof where one slope meets the other.

Ridge board, ridge pole: The timber running along the apex of a roof and sandwiched between the tops of the rafters. A ridge pole is cradled by the ends of the rafters in various ways.

Ridge tile: Angled or half-round tiles to weatherproof the junction between the roof slope coverings at the ridge.

Rietveld, Gerrit Thomas (1888–1964): A leading member of the Dutch Modernist movement De Stijl from 1919. His most famous designs were the Schroeder House at Utrecht in 1924 and his brightly painted angular furniture. His work experienced a big revival in the 1950s.

Riser: The vertical surface of a step or stair.

Riven flagstones: Flagstones that have been split and show a 'riven' face rather than a sawn one.

Rococo: Light and frivolous 18th-century style introduced during the reign of Louis XV to counteract the growing heaviness and pomposity of the Baroque. It was asymmetrical and somewhat abstract, with shell-like forms and many 'C' and 'S' curves, light pastel colours and masses of mirrors lit by candles. Natural rural scenes, flowers, monkeys, branches, trees and chinoiserie were all motifs used by the style, which had success all over Europe, especially in Germany and Austria. French Rococo architecture was known for its grace and delicacy. In England and America it was mostly used in interiors. It had a popular revival in the late 19th century, where it was particularly taken up in the United States.

Romanesque: Style of architecture prevalent in western and southern Europe from the 9th to the 12th century.

Rotunda: A building or room that is circular and often domed.

Roughcast: See **Pebbledash**.

RSJ: Standing for rolled-steel joist, these are strong supports made of rolled steel, generally used to support a ceiling when an opening has to be made in a supporting wall. Once in place, the RSJs are surrounded by plaster or columns to disguise their utilitarian nature.

Running dog: A classical ornament similar to a wave often used in a frieze. It is sometimes called a Vitruvian scroll after the Ancient Roman architect Vitruvius.

Rustic: In the 18th century the basement floor was known as 'the rustic'. In Palladian houses, the lower storey was rusticated and acted as a basement podium for one or more smooth-faced upper storeys.

Rustication: Masonry cut in massive blocks and separated from each other by deep joints. It was used to give a bold texture to exterior walls and particularly to the lower part.

Saltbox: An American term for a house with two storeys in the front and one storey at the back, and a gable roof that extends downwards over the rear of the house.

Sash window: Double-hung window with suspended sashes (the glazed part of a window) opened and closed by a vertical movement.

Schinkel, Karl Friedrich (1781–1841): The greatest German architect of the 19th century and one of the great European Neo-Classical architects in the Grecian mode.

Screed: Layer of mortar used to level up and provide a smooth surface on which to lay finishes like tiles.

Screens passage: The passage formed at the lower end of a medieval hall by screening off the main area from the entrance. It often had a minstrel's gallery over the top for general musical entertainment.

Septic tank: A sealed waterproof tank, usually below ground in country houses that are not on the mains drainage system. Waste material from a drainage system is biologically decomposed before being part-purified and dispersed through a soakaway, which is often constructed in conjunction with the tank.

Shaw, Richard Norman (1831–1912): One of the architects behind the Queen Anne Revival style, which started around 1860.

Shingles: Wooden tiles for covering roofs or the sides of houses (especially in the United States).

Slate hanging: A wall-covering of overlapping rows of slates on a timber sub-structure.

Slips: Well-finished rectangular slabs, usually of marble or slate but sometimes tiled or mirrored, that immediately surround a fireplace opening.

Soane, Sir John (1753–1837): Great late 18th-/early 19th-century British architect. He was superficially a Neo-Classicist but, in fact, he was also an exponent of the Picturesque school. In London he designed the Dulwich College Art Gallery (1811–14) and Saint Peter's church, Walworth, but his most idiosyncratic work was his own house, 13 Lincoln's Inn Fields. This is now the Sir John Soane Museum, with its complicated floor levels, ingenious top lighting and hundreds of mirrors to blur divisions and suggest receding planes.

Soffit: The underside of any architectural element or a band of wood or plaster to hide lights behind. Also called **Intrados**.

Solar: The upper living room in a medieval house, from the Latin *solarium*.

Solarium: A sun terrace, sun roof or loggia.

Spandrel: The triangular area formed between an arch and the rectangle of mouldings in which the arch is placed.

Spire: A tall, pyramidal, polygonal or conical structure rising from a tower, turret or roof – usually of a church – and terminating in a point.

Splat baluster: A staircase baluster cut from a thin board to suggest the design of a conventional baluster in one of the classical shapes, like a barleysugar-twist, vase or column. It was greatly used in the 17th and early 18th centuries, and is not unlike the splat at the back of a Queen Anne chair.

Stile: The outer framing member of a system of panelling, also used in the same way for a panelled door.

Strapwork: Form of decoration in the shape of leather straps originating in the Netherlands around 1540 and brought to Britain via pattern books from the Netherlands and Germany. It is also loosely used to describe Elizabethan and Jacobean ceilings with flat decorated rib-work.

Stretcher: A brick that appears lengthwise on the face of a wall. See also **Header**.

Strings: The two sloping members of a staircase that carry the ends of the treads and the risers.

Strut: A short piece of timber used in old houses to hold two other structural timbers apart.

Stucco: A form of smooth and quite hard rendering, usually painted white or cream, greatly favoured for the walls of early 19th-century and Victorian houses. It was first introduced by the architect John Nash.

Studding: Upright timbers that form the main framework of walls and partitions.

Swag: A decorative garland of flowers, foliage, fruit and so on that looks as if it is suspended between two points.

It is also a term used for curtains when fabric is suspended from both ends of a curtain rod.

Swan neck: A wall coping, pediment or hand rail that adopts an ogee curve.

Tenon: The end of a piece of timber, cut away to fit into a mortise. It is widely used as a framing joint.

Terms: Supports comprising a carved human head and torso, merging into a downward-tapering pedestal.

Tie-beam: A substantial beam spanning the distance from wall to wall that ties together the feet of the principal rafters, thus forming a roof truss.

Tongue-and-groove boarding: Wooden boards in which the protruding edge of one board slots into the edge of the next. It is used primarily for floors but also for ceilings and walls.

Top rail: The uppermost horizontal rail in a system of panelling.

Torus mould: Sometimes called 'bull nose', this is a substantial convex moulding used on steps, sills and the bases of columns.

Transom: Stone or timber members that divide window openings horizontally into separate panes or lights. Transoms above doors serve the same purpose as fanlights.

Truss: Substantial framework of principal rafters for a roof as in a tie-beam or a collar, forming either a triangle or an 'A'.

Tuscan order: The Roman simplification of the Doric column.

Universal beam: Steel support beam, bigger than an RSJ.

Valley: The junction at the internal angle between roof slopes. External junctions are called hip rafters.

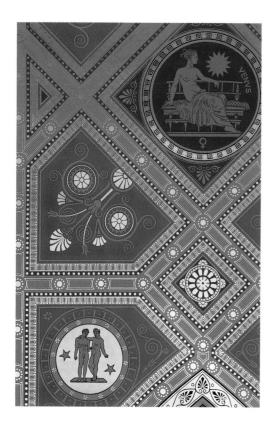

Vanbrugh, Sir John (1664–1726): Multi-talented playwright and the most original English Baroque architect. He switched his talents from drama to house design 'without thought or lecture' said Swift, rather tartly, when he heard that Vanbrugh had been invited by the Earl of Carlisle to try his hand at designing Castle Howard (1699) without any training or qualification. Nevertheless, the house ended up as one of the most famous stately homes in Britain, and Vanbrugh became Christopher Wren's principal colleague. His other great Baroque house is Blenheim Palace.

Venetian window: A window with a rounded arched head that is closely flanked by two smaller and narrower flat-headed windows. Also known as a Palladian window.

Vitruvius: An Ancient Roman architect and theorist who had a huge influence on the Renaissance and then on the 18th century with his book *De Architectura*.

Volute: The distinguishing spiral scroll on an Ionic capital; smaller versions appear on Composite and Corinthian capitals. A key feature of Baroque decoration.

Voysey, Charles F. A. (1857–1941): Arts & Crafts architect, who set up a practice in 1882 and, under the general influence of William Morris, became as interested in design as in architecture. His earliest designs for textiles and wallpapers were in 1883 and his first house commissions date from 1888–9. His many country houses were a great influence on his fellow architects both in Britain and America.

Wagner, Otto (1841–1918): One of the first real Modernists. As early as 1894, when he was Professor of Architecture at the Academy in Vienna, he was pleading for a new approach to architecture, for independence from the past and for Rationalism. ('Nothing that is not practical can be beautiful.') His most amazing work was the Post Office Savings Bank in Vienna. The exterior was faced in marble slabs held in place by aluminium bolts and the interior was topped with a glass barrel vault, not really matched in clarity or economy by anyone else at that date.

Wall-plate: A timber that is laid lengthwise on a wall to receive the ends of the rafters.

Wattle and daub: A method of wall construction consisting of branches or thin laths (wattles) roughly plastered over with mud or clay (daub), often used as a filling between the vertical members of old timber-framed houses.

Weatherboarding: Overlapping horizontal boards covering a timber-framed wall. Also known as clapboard.

Webb, Philip Speakman (1831–1915): English architect who was probably most famous for designing William Morris's Red House, which was made of unadorned red brick. A close friend of Morris, he also designed furniture for Morris's firm.

White, Stanford (1853–1906): American architect and a brilliant and seemingly effortless designer, with a range of work stretching from magazine covers to railway carriages, and from yachts to some of the most original houses of his time.

Wiener Werkstätte: The group (founded in 1903) of talented Viennese architects and designers who were determined Modernists and reformers. Their aim, as was that of William Morris, was to develop more unity between architecture and the crafts. They were also influenced by the work of Charles Rennie Mackintosh, whose furniture and sketches had been exhibited in 1900 at the Vienna Secession.

Wood, John, the elder (1704–54): An English Palladian architect who revolutionized town planning with his scheme for Bath (1727 onwards). He died just after the first stone for the exquisite Bath circus was laid, but his work was carried on by his son, John Wood the younger. He took his father's grand design a step further with the open planning for the magnificent Royal Crescent.

Wren, Sir Christopher (1632–1723): Considered to be the greatest British architect, he was architect to Charles II and designer and rebuilder of Saint Paul's Cathedral, London. Like Vanbrugh, he started off in an entirely different career. Isaac Newton thought him the best geometrician of the day, and in 1657 he was made Professor of Astronomy in London, and Professor of Astonomy at Oxford in 1661. Had he died aged 30 he would have been remembered only as a distinguished figure in British science. After the Great Fire of London in 1666 he was appointed to the commission for the restoration of Saint Paul's and became one of the surveyors under the rebuilding of London Act. In 1669 he became Surveyor General of the King's Work. His first buildings, Pembroke College Chapel and the Sheldonian Theatre, Oxford, were the work of an extraordinarily gifted amateur. But in 1665–6 he spent many months studying French architecture, mostly in Paris, and learnt a very great deal from Le Vau and Mansart. From then on he was greatly influenced by French and Dutch architecture. He built 150 city churches between 1670 and 1686. Apart from Saint Paul's, the grandest and most Baroque of all his work is Greenwich Hospital with its wonderful Painted Hall. Interestingly, although 'Wren' houses were tremendously popular in America, and the idea of them was a central part of the Queen Anne Revival in the late 19th century, no town or country house, apart from the Royal Marlborough House in London, has ever been definitely attributed to him.

Wright, Frank Lloyd (1869–1959): A towering figure among American architects whose work spanned 60 years and was never repetitive or derivative. The first type of building he developed as an independent architect was the Prairie House: low, spreading buildings, with rooms running into each other, terraces merging into gardens and projecting roof lines. Houses of this type are located in the outer suburbs of Chicago like Oak Park and Riverside. The development ended up with houses more daringly original than any other architect of his time. Begun just before 1900, it was finished by 1905. Although Wright consistently went his own way, his house 'Falling Water' in Pennsylvania is closer to the International style than anything else he built, although he greatly influenced Gropius as well as the Dutch De Stijl group.

index

picture credits

The publisher would like to thank the following photographers and organizations for their kind permission to reproduce the photographs in this book.

1 Andreas von Einsiedel; *2 above left* Christian Sarramon (Chateau de Gignac, Provence); *2 below* Michael Donnelly/Elizabeth Whiting & Associates; *4* Per Gunnarsson (Stylist: Susanne Swegen); *5 left* Simon McBride/Interior Archive; *5 right* Simon Upton/ The Interior Archive (Designer: Lisa Bruce/Alvis Vega); *6* Verne Fotografie; *7–8* Richard Powers; *9* Christopher Drake/Red Cover (Designer: Julie Prisca); *10* Gillian Darley/Edifice; *12* Andreas von Einsiedel; *13* Fritz von der Schulenburg/The Interior Archive (Designer: Bruce Oldfield); *14–15* Ray Main/Mainstream; *16 above* Fritz von der Schulenburg/The Interior Archive (Designer: Bruce Oldfield); *16 below–17* Ray Main/Mainstream; *18* Christian Sarramon (Stanton Hall, Louisiana, USA); *19* Christian Sarramon; *20 above* Christian Sarramon (Chateau de Gignac, Normandy); *20 below* Ray Main/ Mainstream; *21* Ray Main/Mainstream (Artist: Michi Uchida); *22* Michael Donnelly/Elizabeth Whiting & Associates; *24* Christopher Drake/Red Cover (Designer: Catherine Memmi); *25* Christian Sarramon; *28* Philippa Lewis/Edifice; *30* Gillian Darley/Edifice; *31* Philippa Lewis/Edifice; *32–33* Caroline Knight/Edifice (Architect: Andrea Palladio); *33* Philippa Lewis/Edifice (Architect: Jacques Sourdeau); *34* Adrian Mayer/Edifice; *35* Philippa Lewis/Edifice; *36* Gillian Darley/Edifice; *37* Andreas von Einsiedel/The National Trust Photographic Library; *38* Philippa Lewis/Edifice; *39* Jan Verlinde; *40* Philippa Lewis/Edifice (Architect: Lord Burlington); *41* Philippa Lewis/Edifice; *42 above* Philippa Lewis/Edifice (Architect: Joseph Collins Wells); *42 below* Philippa Lewis/Edifice (Architect: William Halfpenny); *43* Brian Harrison/Red Cover; *44* Martin Drury/Edifice; *45* Andreas von Einsiedel/The National Trust Photographic Library; *46* Philippa Lewis/Edifice; *47* Philippa Lewis/Edifice (Architect: John Nash); *48 above* Philippa Lewis/Edifice; *48 below* Gillian Darley/ Edifice; *49* Jan Baldwin/Narratives (Architect: M. H. Baillie Scott, Courtesy of the Lakeland Arts Trust); *50* Peter Cook/View (Architect: B Lubetkin); *51* Philippa Lewis/Edifice (Architect: Frank Lloyd Wright); *52* Ray Main/Mainstream (Eltham Palace); *53–54* Gillian Darley/ Edifice; *56* Fritz von der Schulenburg/The Interior Archive; *57* Christian Sarramon; *58* Christopher Drake/ Red Cover; *60 above* Ray Main/Mainstream (Designer: Kelly Hoppen); *60 below* Philippa Lewis/Edifice; *61 left* Philippa Lewis/Edifice; *61 right* Tamsyn Hill/Narratives (Rose Bank Farm, NSW, Australia); *62* Andreas von Einsiedel (Designers: Konstantine & Tomma von Haeften); *63 left* Christian Sarramon; *63 right* Mark Luscombe-Whyte/The Interior Archive; *64 above* Christian Sarramon; *64 below* Philippa Lewis/Edifice; *65* Fritz von der Schulenburg/The Interior Archive (Designer: Catherine Painvin); *66* Richard Bryant/Arcaid (Architect: Raymond McGrath/Munkenbeck & Marshall); *67 left* Benedict Luxmoore/Arcaid (Architect: Marmeduke Smith); *67 right* Christian Sarramon; *68 above* Peter Cook/View (Architect: Frank Lloyd Wright); *68 below* Ray Main/Mainstream; *69 above* Christopher Drake/Red Cover (Designer: Ann Boyd); *69 below* Kristian Septimius Krogh/House of Pictures (stylist: Lise Septimius Krogh, artist Kirsten Thorsted); *70* Julie Phipps/View; *71 above* Angelo Hornak, London; *71 below* Philippa Lewis/Edifice; *72 above* Ray Main/ Mainstream; *72 below* Christian Sarramon; *73* Tamsyn Hill/Narratives (Rose Bank Farm, NSW, Australia); *74 above* Alexander van Berge; *74 below* Luke White/ The Interior Archive; *75–76* Ray Main/Mainstream; *77* Jose van Riele/Marie Claire Maison (Marie Kalt); *78* Caroline Arber/World of Interiors; *80* Verne Fotografie; *82* Nick Kane/Arcaid (David Mikhail Architects); *83* Nick Kane/Arcaid; *84* Alexander van Berge; *85–87* Ray Main/Mainstream; *88* Joe Beynon/ Axiom Photographic Agency; *89 left* Fritz von der Schulenburg/The Interior Archive; *89 right* Joe Cornish/ Arcaid; *90* Angelo Hornak, London; *91 above* Andreas von Einsiedel (Designer: Frank Faulkner); *91 below* Ken Hayden/Red Cover (Designer: Nye Basham); *92* Ray Main/Mainstream; *93* Andreas von Einsiedel (Designer: Frank Faulkner); *94* Andreas von Einsiedel (Designers: Nick and Gabriella Martin); *95 above* Liz Artindale/ Narratives; *95 below* Dominic Blackmore; *96* Ray Main/ Mainstream (Designer: Catherine Memmi); *97* Andreas von Einsiedel (Lulu Guinness); *98–101* Richard Bryant/ Arcaid (Architect: Eva Jiricna); *102* Philippa Lewis/ Edifice; *103 above* Ray Main/Mainstream (20th Century design); *103 below* Tamsyn Hill/Narratives; *104–107* Jean Marc Wullschleger/Tina Hom (Architect: Umberto Prisco); *108* Fritz von der Schulenburg/ The Interior Archive; *110–111* Joe Cornish/Arcaid; *111* Kim Sayer/Edifice; *112–113* Christian Sarramon; *113* Verne Fotografie; *114* Jan Verlinde; *115* Christopher Drake/Red Cover (Designer: Catherine Memmi); *116–119* Brian Harrison/Red Cover; *120 and 121 above* Ray Main/Mainstream; *121 below* Helen Pe/House of Pictures (stylist: Roth & Stone); *122* Andreas von Einsiedel (Architect: Hugh Jacobsen/Eugenie Vorhees); *123* Fritz von der Schulenburg/The Interior Archive; *124–126* Ingalill Snitt; *126 right* Jan Baldwin/Narratives (Designer: Lena Proudlock); *127* Ingalill Snitt; *128–131* Simon Upton/The Interior Archive (Design: Van Breem); *132* Edina van der Wyck/The Interior Archive (Antique dealer: Greville Worthington); *134* Gillian Darley/ Edifice; *135* Philip Bier/View; *136* Simon Upton/Homes & Garden/IPC Syndication; *137* Fritz von der Schulenburg/ The Interior Archive (Design: Catherine Painvin); *138* A. Ianniello/studiopep; *139 left and right* Christian Sarramon; *140* Jan Baldwin/Narratives (Architect: Pierre Lombart); *141* Tim Beddow/The Interior Archive; *142* Ray Main/Mainstream (Artist: Liz Ogden); *142–143* Christian Sarramon; *144–147* Christian Sarramon (Architect: Jean Michel Wilmotte); *148* Fritz von der Schulenburg/The Interior Archive (Design: Anne Vincent); *149* Eugeni Pons/Album; *150* Fritz von der Schulenburg/The Interior Archive; *151 left* Ray Main/Mainstream (John F. Rolf Design and Build); *151 right* Fritz von der Schulenburg/ The Interior Archive; *152–155* Michel Arnaud; *156* Charles French/Axiom Photographic Agency; *158* Verne Fotografie; *159* Chris Coe/Axiom Photographic Agency; *160* Erin Haydn O'Neill/House of Pictures; *161–165* Fritz von der Schulenburg/The Interior Archive; *166 below* Fritz von der Schulenburg/The Interior Archive (Designer: A. Ponchot); *167* Fritz von der Schulenburg/The Interior Archive; *168* Geoff Lung/Vogue Living; *169* Cote Sud/Inside/Red Cover; *170* Ray Main/ Mainstream; *171* Andreas von Einsiedel (Designer: Nick Etherington-Smith); *172–175* Ray Main/Mainstream; *176–183* Richard Powers; *184* Angelo Hornak, London; *187* Ray Main/Mainstream

author's acknowledgments

I would very much like to thank the following people from Conran Octopus who worked with me directly on this book for all their cooperation, patience, good humour, friendliness and sheer hard work: Katey Day, ably assisted by Helen Ridge, who did all the editing; Rachel Davies who found all the pictures; and Mary Staples who did all the design. Also, of course, the Publishing Director, Lorraine Dickey, and Catharine Snow who is not only the marketing *éminence grise* (which could hardly be more important) but, as far as I can see, renowned worldwide in publishing for her niceness. On the American side, I really value the friendship and various talents of Victoria Craven, Anne McNamara and Lee Wiggins at Watson-Guptill. On the personal side, and as usual, my special friends: Virginia Cooper, Kate Coughlan, Anne and Christopher Cruice Goodall, David Gough and Jan Kern, Jim and Judy Lance and Barbara Plumb, who have so generously put up with me writing, sometimes it seems ceaselessly, in their various homes, as well as putting me up and putting up with me in general. Finally, I'd particularly like to thank my daughter, Sophia Gilliatt, for making it possible for me to live so happily and industriously in France.

publisher's acknowledgments

The publisher would like to thank Libby Willis, Emma Clegg and Richard Bird.